THE EFT MANUAL

by Gary Craig

Energy Psychology Press
Santa Rosa, CA 95403
www.energypsychologypress.com

Cataloging-in-Publication Data

Craig, Gary, 1940–
The EFT manual / Gary Craig. — 1st ed.
    p. cm.
Includes bibliographical references and index.
ISBN 978-1-60415-030-8
1. Emotion-focused therapy. I. Title.
RC489.F62C73 2008
616.89'14—dc22

2008012258

This book demonstrates an impressive personal improvement tool. It is not a substitute for training in psychology or psychotherapy. Nothing contained herein is meant to replace qualified medical advice. The author urges the reader to use these techniques under the supervision of a qualified therapist or physician. The author and publisher do not assume responsibility for how the reader chooses to apply the techniques herein.

Cover design by Victoria Valentine
Editing by Stephanie Marohn
Typesetting by Karin Kinsey
Typeset in Cochin and Adobe Garamond
Printed in USA by Bang Printing
First Edition

10 9 8 7 6 5 4 3 2 1

Contents

Acknowledgments vii

Introduction: Entry to a Palace of
    Healing Possibilities xi

A Note to Therapists, Physicians, Ministers, and
    Other Members of the Healing Professions xvi

A Common Sense Approach xvii

The Easy Way to Use This Book xix

EFT Part I

Chapter 1: What to Expect from EFT
    and This Book 25

Emotional Freedom 25

Simplicity 27

Healthy Skepticism 27

Case Histories 32

Repetition 33

Chapter 2: The Science Behind EFT 35

    An Engineer Looks
        at the Science of Psychology 35

    The Body's Energy System 42

    Dr. Callahan's First Experience.................................. 44

    The Discovery Statement 45

    The 100% Overhaul Concept..................................... 51

Chapter 3: The Basic Recipe.................................... 53

    Like Baking a Cake 53

    Ingredient #1: The Setup... 54

    Ingredient #2: The Sequence....................................... 62

    Ingredient #3: The 9 Gamut Procedure........................ 70

    Ingredient #4: The Sequence (Again)........................... 72

    The Reminder Phrase 72

    Subsequent Round Adjustments................................. 76

Chapter 4: Tips on How to Apply EFT 79

    Testing 80

    Aspects.. 81

    Persistence Pays.. 83

    Be Specific When Possible.. 84

    The Generalization Effect.. 85

    Try It on Everything.. 86

    EFT in a Nutshell 87

    Quick Guide to EFT.. 88

Chapter 5: Frequently Asked Questions....................... 91

Chapter 6: Case Histories.. 101

Case History #1: Fear of Public Speaking 102

Case History #2: Asthma 103

Case History #3: Sexual Abuse 104

Case History #4: Anxiety and Fingernail Biting......... 105

Case History #5: Fear of Spiders 106

Case History #6: Coffee Addiction 107

Case History #7: Alcoholism 108

Case History #8: Grief 109

Case History #9: Fear of Needles 110

Case History #10: Addiction to Peanut M&M's 110

Case History #11: Physical Pain.................................. 111

Case History #12: Low Back Pain 112

Case History #13: Guilt and Insomnia......................... 112

Case History #14: Constipation.................................... 113

Case History #15: Body Embarrassment..................... 114

Case History #16: Lupus 115

Case History #17: Ulcerative Colitis 117

Case History #18: Panic Attack.................................... 117

Case History #19: Fear of Elevators 118

EFT Part II

Chapter 7: The Impediments to Perfection................. 123

Aspects.. 123

Psychological Reversal 124

Collarbone Breathing Problem 132

Energy Toxins 134

The Value of Persistence 141

Chapter 8: Shortcuts 143

Shortening the Sequence 144

Eliminating the Setup 145

Eliminating the 9 Gamut Procedure 146

The Floor to Ceiling Eye Roll 146

The Art of Doing Shortcuts 147

Appendices

Appendix A: Articles by Gary Craig 151

Using EFT on Fears and Phobias 151

Using EFT on Traumatic Memories 157

Using EFT for Addictions 161

Using EFT for Physical Healing 177

Using EFT to Enhance Your Self-Image 183

Appendix B: A Format Diagram for Using EFT 191

Appendix C: Summary of
the EFT Videos and Audios 193

The Videos on DVD for Part I 193

The Videos on DVD for Part II 197

The Audio Recordings on DVD for Part I 202

Acknowledgments

We are on the ground floor of a healing high-rise. That high-rise is the field of energy psychology. Unfortunately, we will never meet some of the benefactors who made this building possible because their essential contributions were made more than five thousand years ago. These brilliant people discovered, and mapped, the subtle energies that course throughout the body. These subtle energies became the centerpiece of the healing modality called acupuncture, which is still used around the world today. As the subtle energies are also the centerpiece of Emotional Freedom Techniques (EFT), this new modality and acupuncture are cousins.

In more recent times, other dedicated souls advanced our use of the ancient healing techniques. Principal among them is Dr. George Goodheart who made many fine contributions to the field of applied kinesiology, a forerunner of EFT.

Dr. John Diamond's work gets exceptional applause because, to my knowledge, he was one of the first psychiatrists to use, and write about, these subtle energies. His many pioneering concepts, together with the advanced ideas from applied kinesiology, formed the foundation on which the new healing high-rise is being constructed.

Dr. Roger Callahan, from whom I received my original introduction to the energy tapping procedures that prompted me to develop EFT, deserves all the credit history can give him. He was first to bring this methodology to the public in a substantial way and did so despite open hostility from his own profession, the field of psychology. As you might appreciate, it takes heavy doses of conviction to plow through the ingrained beliefs of conventional thinking. Without Dr. Callahan's missionary drive, we might still be sitting around theorizing about this "interesting thing."

It is on the foundation laid by these giants that I humbly add to the building. My own contribution to the rapidly expanding energy psychology field has been to reduce the unnecessary complexity that inevitably finds its way into new discoveries. My contribution, EFT, is an elegantly simple version of energy tapping procedures that professionals and laypeople alike can use on a wide variety of problems.

Being on the ground floor of this new healing high-rise, we have much to learn. Accordingly, I am indebted to the many EFT practitioners who tirelessly contribute their innovations to our website (www.emofree.com). They are taking us to new levels.

Gary Craig

Introduction:
Entry to a Palace of
Healing Possibilities

As I write this I'm home alone on a Tuesday evening. There's a light rain outside making gentle noises on the window. After two years of writing and filming, the Emotional Freedom Techniques (EFT) course, which includes this manual along with videos and audio recordings (see appendix C), is complete. Five minutes ago the tears came rolling down my face. At that moment I knew why I authored this course. What I mean is, I always knew why, but I didn't know how to say it. Now I can put it in words. Here's the story.

Five minutes ago I was reviewing a video that my associate, Adrienne Fowlie, and I made at the Veterans Administration in Los Angeles ("6 Days at the VA"; see appendix C). We spent six days there using EFT to help Vietnam vets get beyond the horrible memories of war. They had posttraumatic stress disorder (PTSD), which is among the most severe forms of emotional disorders known. Every day these men relive the catastrophes of war, such as being forced to shoot innocent civilians (including young children), burying people in open trenches, and watching their own dear friends die or become dismembered. The sounds of gunfire, bombs, and screams ricochet in their heads day and night. They sweat. They cry. They have headaches and anxiety attacks. They are depressed and in pain. They have fears and phobias and are afraid to go to sleep at night because of their nightmares. Sometimes only drugs ease the ever-present horror of war. Many of the vets had been in therapy for twenty years—with little relief.

I still remember how thrilled I was when the VA invited Adrienne and me to bring EFT to our soldiers. They gave us free rein to counsel with these men in any way we wanted. This would be the ultimate test of the power of EFT. If all it did was make a modest, but notice-able, difference in the lives of these severely disabled men, most people would have considered it successful. In fact, it did much more.

The VA didn't pay us. They didn't have a budget for outside help like this. In fact, we had to pay for our own airfare, hotel bills, meals, and car rentals. But we didn't care. We would have paid much more just for the opportunity.

The video I was watching was a summary of what happened during those six days. One section was all about Rich, who had been in therapy for seventeen years for his PTSD. The symptoms that plagued him were: more than one hundred haunting war memories, many of which he relived daily; a major height phobia, aggravated by having made more than fifty parachute jumps; and insomnia that kept him trying for three or four hours to get to sleep every night, even under strong medication. After using EFT with him, every trace of these problems vanished.

Like most people, Rich had a hard time believing that these rather strange-appearing procedures would work. But he was willing to give them a try. We started with his height phobia. After about fifteen minutes with EFT, it was gone. He tested it by going several stories up in a building and looking down over a fire escape. To his amazement, he had no phobic reaction. We then applied EFT to several of his most intense war memories and neutralized all of them within an hour. He still remembers them, of course, but they no longer have any emotional charge.

We taught the techniques to Rich (just as you are being taught through this manual) so he could work on his own on the rest of his war memories. Within a few days they were all neutralized. They no longer bothered him. As a result the insomnia went away and so did the insomnia medication (under the supervision of his physician). Two months later I spoke with Rich on the phone. He was still free of the problems.

That's real emotional freedom. It's the end of years of torment. It's like walking out of a prison. And I had the privilege of handing him the keys. What a feeling!

This is the promise of EFT. Master it and you can do for yourself, and others, what happened for Rich.

Then there were Robert, Gary, Phillip, and Ralph, all of whom had traumatic war memories. In minutes, EFT provided relief for the memories we worked on. To see the smiles and hear the gratitude was a form of joy that only tears can express.

Then came the video interview with Anthony. He was so frightened by his war experiences that he was afraid to go into a public place, such as a restaurant, for fear a Vietnamese soldier would come in firing an AK-47. He would freeze up at the mere thought of it. He knew, of course, it wasn't logical, but that didn't make the fear any less. That's what PTSD is like.

After using EFT, Anthony went with us to a crowded restaurant and, in his words, "didn't have a nickel's worth of anxiety." The three of us (Adrienne, Anthony, and I) casually joked and laughed while we had a leisurely dinner in this restaurant, crowded with more than two hundred people. Anthony was completely relaxed. The fear was gone. Again, what a feeling it was to be able to make such a difference in someone's life.

Then, in the interview on camera, he paused for a moment before saying, "God has blessed me, I swear. I think it was my time to meet you guys."

Watching the video of him, there in my living room, happy tears rolled down my face.

The human value in EFT deserves its own mountaintop.

Now you can understand my motivation for writing this manual. It is because God has blessed me, I swear. It is my time to meet you!

Together we will build within you a bridge to the land of personal peace. Once built, this bridge will become a lifetime skill that you can use to spread emotional freedom, and joy, from yourself to others. And it's permanent. Like gold, it doesn't rust or tarnish or become obsolete. It will always be there for you.

> Together we will build within you a bridge
> to the land of personal peace.

You and I are about to travel together on a journey toward emotional freedom. It will be like nothing you have experienced before, I promise. It is not a mythical ride on a magic carpet that ends in illusion. It is a real ride destined to give you real results, just as it did our veterans. You will, indeed, develop the ability to discard your fears, phobias, traumatic memories, anger, guilt, grief, and all other limiting emotions. And it won't take years and years of painstakingly slow and financially draining sessions either. Often, even the most severe negative emotions vanish in minutes.

Master what's in these pages and you will never view healing the same way again because of this time differential and the fact that, for a wide variety of people and issues, persistent use of EFT often produces results when nothing else will.

Further, physicians acquainted with EFT will likely think twice before recommending drugs, surgeries, radiation, and the like as the first intervention in physical health problems. "Why not try EFT first?" is the question often echoed by those familiar with this intriguing process. Those who have experience with EFT know that profound physical healings often take place during its application. Vision has improved, headaches have disappeared, and cancer pains and symptoms have subsided. The reason for this is that EFT addresses causes that Western healing practices have largely ignored: emotions and the disruptions in the body's energy meridians. These causes, of course, are the centerpiece of EFT, as you will learn in this book.

This book stresses the emotional healings and doesn't cover the physical healings in nearly as dramatic a fashion as they actually occur. This is because it is the emotional and energetic underpinnings of all disorders, whether the manifestation is emotional or physical, that we need to understand and address. As a reminder of EFT's wide application, I sprinkle reference to the physical healings throughout this manual. EFT is not meant, however, to replace qualified medical advice.

A Note to Therapists, Physicians, Ministers, and Other Members of the Healing Professions

This manual represents a radical departure from conventional techniques. Properly used, it should multiply your abilities severalfold. Since the book is for professionals and laypeople alike, I have taken pains to present this remarkable healing tool in a practical way and have purposely avoided the somewhat stodgy, hard to understand presentation of an official textbook. The accuracy and completeness demanded by the professional has been maintained, however, albeit amidst analogies and user-friendly graphics. This presentation is unconventional, of course, but so is Emotional Freedom Techniques. If you are looking for convention, you came to the wrong place.

A Common Sense Approach

Common sense suggests that you wouldn't expect much in the way of negative side effects from EFT. This is because there are:

- No surgical procedures
- No needles
- No pills or chemicals
- No pushing or pulling on the body

Instead, there are just a few seemingly harmless procedures that involve tapping, humming, counting, and rolling your eyes around in your head. One of the delightful aspects of EFT (and its many cousins) is that, for the vast majority of people, it can be applied with little or no pain. As a result of this and its simple application, therapists are routinely teaching the process to their clients for use at home; teachers are learning it for use with their students; coaches are learning it for use with their athletes; parents are learning it for use with their children; physicians are learning it for pain management with their patients; massage practitioners are blending it with their existing procedures for longer and more lasting results; spiritual leaders are applying it to those in need; and chiropractors, acupuncturists, and homeopaths are augmenting their practices and teaching it to patients for self-use.

By now more than one million people have used EFT and the number of complaints are well under 1 percent.

Once in a while someone might report feeling a little nauseous and, on occasion, a few people report "feeling worse." Because these reports are so infrequent it is unknown whether EFT actually caused the problem. Some people, by the way, feel nauseous or "get worse" at the mere mention of their particular problem. They will do so whether or not EFT is introduced.

EFT is still in its beginning stages, however, and we have much to learn. Thus it is possible that using EFT could be deleterious to someone. Accordingly, you should use EFT with appropriate caution. While fascination with these procedures gives much cause for enthusiasm, you must weigh that enthusiasm against some common sense caveats.

First, do *not* apply it to people with serious issues unless you have the appropriate experience to do so. Some people have been so badly traumatized and/or abused that they have developed severe psychological problems, such as multiple personalities, paranoia, schizophrenia, and other serious mental disorders. Although EFT has been helpful even in such severe cases, only qualified professionals with experience in these disorders should use it with this population. The reason is that some of these patients experience "abreactions" to EFT, wherein they go out of control. During abreactions they can be harmful to themselves and others and may need to be sedated or hospitalized. This, obviously, is no place for the novice—no matter how enthusiastic you might be with the tapping procedures. Incidentally, we don't yet know whether tapping actually causes such abreactions or if it is just the individual's memory of troublesome issues that precipitates such problems. Nonetheless, if you have no experience in these areas, please don't go where you don't belong.

Second, on some occasions, people undergoing EFT have normal tears or other forms of distress that accompany the recalling of their troublesome memories. On other occasions, some physical pains "get worse," at least temporarily. The proficient and experienced professional will greet these responses as normal and appropriately apply EFT for their resolution. Again, when these responses occur, common sense must prevail. If you the EFTer get in over your head when applying EFT to yourself or someone else, seek the help of an experienced EFT practitioner.

The Easy Way to Use This Book

Be sure to read this section. It will save you time and increase your efficiency with EFT.

It is understandably human (I'm guilty of this too) for newcomers to glance at this manual to get a few highlights and then dive directly into the case histories. If you are serious about learning how to do EFT, it is important to read this manual sequentially. For example, the short-cuts discussed in Part II, which can cut treatment time by more than 50 percent, are based on concepts detailed earlier in the book, which you will not understand unless you have absorbed the material sequentially. Further, important terms such as "aspects," "psychological reversal," and "energy toxins" cannot be properly understood without the requisite background. For these reasons, I strongly suggest that you (even if you are an experienced therapist) read the material in the order it is presented. That's actually the easy way. Reading it out of order is the hard way.

So to learn EFT the easy way, first read Part I, going through the sections in order. The main chapter in Part I, "The Basic Recipe," covers in detail EFT's fundamental healing routine and is the pad from which everything else in EFT is launched. As you will learn in Part II, however, you rarely need to do the entire Basic Recipe. Various shortcuts almost always suffice. Nonetheless, you need to know the full Basic Recipe as a foundation before you can implement the shortcuts and master the art of EFT.

When you are ready, go on to Part II, proceeding through the sections in order as you did in Part I. Here you will be introduced to the impediments to perfection (including energy toxins), shortcuts, and other helpful tips for getting the most out of EFT.

In the appendices, you will find articles by the author, a format diagram for using EFT, and summaries of the video and audio recordings that augment this manual to provide a more comprehensive EFT course (available at www.emofree.com). This manual teaches all the basics, whereas the videos and audios give you a visual/auditory experience of EFT in action and help you expand your skills. I highly recommend that you complete all aspects of the course, rather than merely reading this book. The reason is that, while EFT is simple to use once mastered, your skills and the ensuing results will be improved with the more training and practice you have.

EFT Part I

This part of the book covers the basics of Emotional Freedom Techniques (EFT) and a step-by-step procedure for putting it into action. Shortcuts and other advanced concepts are presented in Part II. Part I needs to be mastered first.

1

What to Expect from
EFT and This Book

Emotional Freedom — Simplicity — Healthy Skepticism —
Case Histories — Repetition

Emotional Freedom

Perhaps I should be a bit more humble about it, but
I think EFT will dramatically change your world. I will
go further and say that these techniques might compete
in importance with the Declaration of Independence.
For some, they are the Declaration of Independence. By
"independence," I mean:

- Freedom from negative emotions, that is, freedom that
  allows you to blossom and rise above whatever hidden
  hurdles keep you from performing to your capacity.

- Freedom from years of self-doubt or grief over the
  loss of a loved one, or anger, or negative memories
  involving rape or other forms of abuse.

- Freedom to earn that greater income, make those business calls, start that new business, improve your golf score, lose that weight, approach people with ease, or become a public speaker, singer, or comedian.

- Freedom from the anxiety that causes you to take those pills, drink that alcohol, smoke those cigarettes, or raid that refrigerator.

- Freedom to express love easily and walk upon this planet with grace and confidence.

- Freedom from intense fears or phobias or anxiety or panic attacks or posttraumatic stress disorder (PTSD) or addictive cravings or depression or guilt... or...or...or...

As I said in the introduction, I think EFT will dramatically change your world. There is no long, drawn-out, "tell me your life story" feature to EFT. There are no pills. There is no painful reliving of past traumatic events. It doesn't take months or years but, rather, only a fraction of the time typically required in conventional psychotherapy—it is often done in minutes. People simply get beyond their emotional luggage, usually permanently, and go about their lives more effectively.

EFT is based on the discovery that imbalances in the body's energy system have profound effects on one's personal psychology. Correcting these imbalances, which is done by tapping on certain body locations, often leads to rapid remedies. By rapid, I mean, most of the problems vanish in minutes. This is demonstrated repeatedly in the case histories in this manual. A few problems take longer, maybe two or three brief sessions. The most difficult ones tend to require anywhere from a few days to several weeks. Fortunately, those are in the minority.

Simplicity

This manual does not purport to teach you every intricacy regarding these discoveries. That would take hundreds of pages and require you to delve into such highly technical areas as quantum physics and morphogenetic fields. I cut through all of that here and provide a simple, highly workable version for the everyday citizen.

Learning EFT is like learning to drive a car. You don't have to know all the physics, chemistry, engineering, and mathematics of an automobile in order to learn how to drive it. But you do need to know about the gas pedal, the brake, the steering wheel, and the gearshift. With those basics you can drive on most roads with ease.

My purpose here is to reduce a complex subject to a few simple, easy to understand procedures (gas pedal, brake, etc.). The shorter and more concise I can make them, the easier they will be to learn and use. Accordingly, this book is peppered with easy to grasp examples, pictures, and analogies so that every piece of the EFT process will be clear and obvious.

Healthy Skepticism

A new innovation usually meets with skepticism because it violates people's beliefs. And EFT flies in the face of just about every belief there is about psychology and emotional healing. Rapid remedies for "difficult" emotional problems are, in some circles, considered impossible and anyone who purports to do them rapidly is labeled a charlatan. "After all," the belief goes, "these things are deeply ingrained in people and therefore they must take a long time to remedy."

Beliefs are very powerful. We fight wars over them. We build monuments to them. Medicine, psychology, and political systems are built on them. But, alas, sometimes they aren't true. We just think they are.

If your reaction to the promises made in the preceding pages includes an "it's too good to be true" attitude or anything like that, then I have probably already violated your beliefs. This is healthy and to be expected. New ideas should be subject to rigorous scrutiny. It lends them strength in the long run.

What you have here is a major innovation. As you will see, EFT is based on the soundest of scientific principles. But because it is so dramatically different from "conventional wisdom," it is consistently, and understandably, greeted with skepticism. EFT is not alone in this. Other innovations have met with similar attitudes. Here are a few quotes from history:

"Heavier-than-air flying machines are impossible."

—Lord Kelvin, President of the Royal Society, 1895

"Everything that can be invented has been invented."

—Charles H. Duell, Director of U.S. Patent Office, 1899

"Sensible and responsible women do not want to vote."

—Grover Cleveland, 1905

"There is no likelihood man can ever tap the power of the atom."

—Robert Millikan, Nobel Laureate in Physics, 1923

"Who the heck wants to hear actors talk?"

—Harry M. Warner, Warner Bros. Pictures, 1927

But even if you have no skepticism regarding EFT, I guarantee that you will run into major skepticism from others that you try to help with it. How do I know this? Years of experience. This skepticism is not to be criticized, however. But it does need to be understood because there are some unique features to it regarding EFT.

Here's an example. On many occasions I have demonstrated these techniques (to newcomers) from the stage with five or ten volunteers from the audience. Within a few minutes at least 80 percent of them have obvious major reduction, or outright elimination, of physical and emotional problems. Fears subside, headaches go away, breathing clears, and emotional trauma disappears. I then ask the audience, "Who here is skeptical about this?" Invariably, at least half of the hands go up.

I then ask them if they think the changes these people made were real and they agree that the changes were real. After all, the people who made the changes are usually friends of the audience and strangers to me. The other audience members know that the volunteer subjects are reporting honestly. " So why are you skeptical?" I ask. And then I get a barrage of reasons as to why it worked, such as:

- I am told that I hypnotized the people. This is interesting because I don't know the first thing about hypnosis—and neither do the people who propose this reason.

- I am told that it is just positive thinking, even though no one has ever seen positive thinking make these kinds of changes this fast.

- I am told that the people just wanted to get over their problems. It was simply a case of "mind over matter." Then why didn't they get over the problems before they came on stage?

- I am told that it won't last because there is no such thing as a quick fix. Yet they take drugs like penicillin to "quick fix" other ailments.

- I am told that the tapping techniques were distractions that took people's minds off their problems. This ignores the requirement that people tune in to their problem for EFT to work. It is the exact opposite of distraction.

Now here's what's really fascinating about this phenomenon: None of the reasons given include EFT. EFT is somehow excluded from the list of possibilities.

What an odd reaction. You would think that people, after seeing these unmistakable benefits, would bombard me with questions as to how the techniques worked so they could better understand the process. Instead, they tend to ignore the process and offer other explanations. They don't ask me what happened. They tell me instead.

They each reach into their own bag of knowledge and experience and link what just happened to what they already "know" to be true. EFT isn't in that bag (yet) and so they have difficulty making the link. Now I know how our scientists of several centuries ago felt when they tried to tell flat-earth believers that the world was round.

People from all walks of life respond this way. It doesn't matter whether they are bus drivers or PhDs. Even some of my closest friends have simply "explained away" these stunning results and snicker a bit at the "silliness" of the process.

Hardly ever does anyone say to me, "Oh, it's like you said. You balanced their energy system while they were tuned in to the problem and thereby eliminated the cause." Yet that is what happened. And it is exactly what I spent the previous half hour telling the audience would happen. It is the only thing that happened during the few minutes these people were on stage and it is the only thing that brought about the changes.

Often, even the people making the changes will credit something else for creating the change. And it's usually something totally unrelated, like a recent earthquake or a raise in pay they just received. Mind you, they don't deny the change occurred or that it happened while doing EFT. They just aren't able to link it with the tapping techniques. To them it doesn't compute. It doesn't make sense. There must be some other explanation, or so they think.

This is not to be criticized, but it is important to observe and understand because it happens with great frequency. In fact, most people experience it, and there is a high likelihood you will be among them. That's why I am telling you this. If you are not aware of this tendency, you may explain away EFT and turn your back on your ticket to emotional freedom and all the lifetime benefits it offers.

Another reason for skepticism is that EFT looks weird. These techniques will have you talking to yourself, rolling your eyes around in your head, and humming a song while tapping on various parts of your body. They don't even remotely resemble the practice of psychology as most people know it, and may be way outside your belief system. Once you understand the logic behind them, however, these techniques become obvious. And you may wonder why they weren't discovered earlier.

That being said, here's an interesting aside. You do not have to believe in these techniques for them to work. Some people mistakenly conclude that EFT gets results simply because people believe in it. The fact is that people rarely believe in these techniques at first. They are almost always skeptical, at least to a degree. Despite the usual lack of belief by newcomers, the results obtained by EFT occur undiminished. People make their improvements in spite of their skepticism.

Case Histories

As a child I was quite taken by the game of baseball and I used to dream about playing center field for the New York Yankees. Batting looked so easy—just stand up there at the plate and hit the ball when it is thrown to you. Hitting baseballs, of course, is a skill and it takes experience to become proficient at it. The more fastballs, curves, and sliders you face, the better you become. The same is true with EFT.

Memorizing the mechanics of EFT is easy. Applying it is almost as easy, and you can become proficient with the mechanics after only a handful of tries. If you wish to master it, however, you will need to study diligently and use it on a wide variety of problems (fastballs, curves, and sliders) to perfect your skill. In short, you will need more training and experience than what you are receiving with this manual alone.

Perhaps the biggest limit you will encounter in using EFT is not recognizing how much you can do with it. That is one of the reasons this manual features an array of case histories. You will read about some people getting over lifelong problems in moments while others require persistence or achieve only partial relief. The cases give you the spectrum of actual experience. The case histories also illustrate that EFT is everything I say it is — and more.

Repetition

I am a great believer in repetition. It is the most time-honored teaching tool, and I use it relentlessly. The more you are exposed to something, the better you learn it. That's why you will hear me come at these ideas from numerous different angles in this book. I visit the same concepts repeatedly. If you grow weary of hearing an idea, be thankful. That means you have learned it so well that it now bores you a bit. That is far better than being exposed to an idea only once and not having it take root in your memory. Given the major importance of these techniques to the quality of your life, I do you a shameful disservice if I don't drum these crucial ideas home.

Note: Please recall that the emotional and energetic releases brought about by EFT frequently result in profound physical healings.

2

The Science
Behind EFT

An Engineer Looks at the Science of Psychology —
The Body's Energy System — Dr. Callahan's First
Experience — The Discovery Statement — The 100%
Overhaul Concept

An Engineer Looks at the Science of Psychology

This book is written by a Stanford engineer. I am not
a psychologist with a long list of initials behind my name.
People call me Gary and not Dr. so and so. If you are a
conventional thinker, that might bother you. After all,
what business does an engineer have intruding into the
field of psychology? The physical sciences and the mind
sciences appear to have nothing in common.

But forty years ago I realized that the quality of a
person's life is directly related to a person's emotional
health. Emotional health is the foundation beneath self-
confidence, and self-confidence is the springboard to

achievement in every walk of life. This is not a new idea, of course. Virtually everyone agrees with it and the self-help section in every major bookstore is burgeoning with books on the subject. Most people take this idea for granted and read a book or attend a seminar on it now and then. But I took it seriously—very seriously. My view was that as long as I was going to spend decades on this planet, I might as well make it a joyous experience for myself and others. So I went on a forty-year search to find tools that would help people in this regard.

I read all those books (by the hundreds) and spent thousands of dollars on seminars and tapes. I chased down every lead I could find with the enthusiasm of a newspaper reporter on the hunt for that "big story." I talked to psychiatrists, psychologists, and psychotherapists of every kind to find what worked. And EFT, by far, is the most fascinating, most rewarding, most effective tool I have ever found for personal improvement. It lives up to its name and does, indeed, provide freedom from negative emotions.

But I'm getting ahead of myself. I want to cover some of the milestones of my search because they form the important base on which to build your introduction to this ingenious discovery.

First, please understand that I have never formally used my training as an engineer. I have always chosen people-oriented professions and have, at the same time, always pursued my true passion as a personal performance coach. But that doesn't mean my scientific training didn't influence me. Indeed, that training led me to many useful personal performance tools. You see, engineering is an exact science. It is very practical. Two plus two must equal four. There is a reason for everything. Logic tends to rule in the thinking of an engineer. When I set out to find personal improvement tools, I took that mindset with me. To me a tool had to make sense, it had to be practical, and it had to be scientific. In short, if it didn't work in the real world, I wasn't interested.

So I began reading books and attending seminars on psychology. It was the "logical" thing to do. But psychology was a puzzle to me. I was looking for the same logic and precision that I was used to as an engineer, but it didn't seem to be there. After many years of probing the institution known as psychology, I can assure you that the science of engineering and the science of psychology bear little relationship to each other.

On the surface, psychology seems to be quite scientific. There are laboratories in nearly every major university in America dedicated to research on psychological issues. Theories are put forward and rigorously tested. "Controlled" studies are done to assure the findings are valid. These studies then form the basis of carloads of professional papers written by the most highly esteemed practitioners in the field. It all seems very impressive and, in many ways, it is.

All this research does uncover much valuable information on aspects of our thinking process and our behaviors. This information is used effectively in sales and advertising and many other fields. But the vast majority of the research findings have not led to the development of therapeutic techniques that give people rapid, long-lasting relief from their emotional problems. This statement may sound a bit irreverent, but I mean no disrespect. By an engineer's standards, the statement is true. There are some exceptions, of course, but the vast majority of the conventional techniques have poor track records.

This is not a criticism of psychotherapists. I find the members of that profession to be among the most dedicated people on Earth and I count many of them as my personal friends. They are very caring individuals who have great concern for their patients. They work long hours and are constantly seeking new ways to improve on the tools of their trade.

EFT is a new tool for their "people-helping toolbox" that contains a distinctly scientific component. That scientific component would satisfy even the most demanding engineer. The component is: The technique, practiced correctly, has to improve any therapist's performance.

Some people undergo therapy for months or years for relief from their fears, anger, guilt, grief, depression, traumatic memories, and so on, and make little or no headway. So they switch therapists in hopes that someone else has "the answer." The results are often the same. They switch again...and again...and again. They spend money. They spend time. They go through emotionally painful sessions. But if anything positive happens for most of these people, it doesn't appear to be much.

In my investigation, I found this fact rather curious. To me there was something obviously wrong with the methods used because (1) they weren't working (at least by my standards), and (2) they were painfully slow. So I asked therapists and patients, "Why does it take so long to do so little?" The answers varied, of course, but generally speaking they went something like this:

- "Well, the problem is deeply ingrained" or
- "It is a deep scar" or
- "We don't know for sure. We are dealing with the mysteries of the mind, you know."

My engineering mind tossed these answers out immediately as convenient ways to explain away, or rationalize, methods that just didn't do much. But to most people the methods sounded good. They sounded reasonable. So they were accepted and pursued. Besides, what else could be done? Real answers weren't available.

I also don't mean to imply here that no one gets any help or relief from therapy. That just isn't so. Some do. But in general, conventional psychotherapy is among the slowest, most ineffective sciences on Earth.

To this engineer the only scientific laboratory that counts is the real world and there is only one criterion for whether a given psychological theory is valid, and that is: Does it work for the client?

If an engineer designs a computer, for example, it had better work in the real world and work perfectly. Otherwise, consumers will return it promptly for a refund and may send a nasty letter to boot. In emotional health, however, if a new method seems to work once in a while (and as long as it is not too radical), it is often heralded as a breakthrough and the discoverer of the method gets rich by writing books and giving lectures.

In the early years of my search for personal improvement tools, I considered getting degrees in psychology. But the more I was exposed to that field, the more I concluded that to do so would work to my disadvantage. Why? Because I would have to learn about methods that didn't work, at least by my standards.

I just couldn't see the merit in going through all that schooling to learn something that, to me, was of questionable value. It would, paradoxically, distract me from my true goal of finding personal improvement tools that work.

As the years went by I discovered a list of helpful tools that I used for myself and taught to others. None of them, incidentally, came from psychology textbooks. They were all well received and effective when properly applied.

One of the tools that I thought was quite helpful was Neuro-Linguistic Programming (NLP). I dove into that headfirst and became quite proficient at it. I became certified as a master practitioner and helped a lot of people with it. I recommend its study to anyone who is interested in personal improvement.

Then my search for reliable personal improvement tools took a mega jump when I heard about a psychologist in southern California, Dr. Roger Callahan, who was giving people relief from intense fears (phobias) in minutes. Ever the eager beaver, I called him immediately to inquire about his approach. He told me that his method wasn't limited to phobias but applied to all negative emotions. That included depression, guilt, anger, grief, posttraumatic stress disorder (PTSD), and any other negative emotion I could name. Furthermore, the method usually only took minutes to perform and the result was usually permanent.

Though I was enthusiastic about his claims, I must admit to a fair amount of skepticism as well. The statement sounded a bit grandiose, but I kept listening. He went on to say that the method consisted of tapping with the fingertips at the end points of the body's energy meridians.

"You mean meridians like in acupuncture?" I asked.

"Exactly," he replied.

"Hmm," I thought, "that's a little far out."

Here was a clinical psychologist making some startling claims and trying to explain them in terms of the subtle amounts of electricity that circulate throughout the body. Psychology and electricity seemed rather far apart to me, but I bought some of his videos anyway so I could see a demonstration.

I was stunned by what I saw. Clearly and obviously, people were getting beyond the most intense of emotions, they were doing so in moments, and the results were long lasting. I had never seen anything close to this — anywhere.

I still didn't see the connection between emotions and the body's energy system, but it did have a scientific ring to me. Perhaps I was about to find a truly scientific approach to psychology.

Indeed, that is what I found. The true cause of negative emotions, it turns out, is not where everyone thinks it is. It is not where psychologists have been looking. That's why they haven't found it. The cause of all negative emotions can be found in the body's energy system. This is an important, paradigm-shifting concept. The concept may seem strange to you, but the proof is in the results. As I said, the only laboratory that counts is the real world and that is where these techniques excel. The speed, efficiency, and long-lasting nature of these techniques are far beyond anything I have come across in forty years of intensive searching.

The body's energy system is the engine that runs EFT, so to build your understanding of the method, we need to focus a bit on this vital system.

The Body's Energy System

Our bodies have a profound electrical nature. Any beginning course in anatomy covers this. Shuffle your feet across a carpet and then touch an item made of metal. Sometimes you can see the static electricity that is discharged from your fingertip. This wouldn't be possible unless your body had an electrical nature.

If you touch a hot stove, you will feel the pain instantly because it is electrically transmitted along the nerves to your brain. The pain travels at the speed of electricity and that is why you feel pain so quickly. Electrical messages are constantly sent throughout your body to keep it informed of what is going on. Without this energy flow, you would not be able to see, hear, feel, taste, or smell.

Other forms of evidence of the existence of electricity (energy) in the body are the electroencephalograph (EEG) and electrocardiograph (EKG). The EEG records the electrical activity of the brain and the EKG records the electrical activity of the heart. These devices have been used by medical science for decades and are the ones you see in TV hospital dramas hooked up to dying patients. When the screen stops "blipping," the patient is dead.

Our electrical systems are vital to our physical health. What could be more obvious? When the energy stops flowing, we die. Ask your doctor about this. No one disputes it. In fact, civilization has known about this for millennia. About five thousand years ago, the Chinese discovered a complex system of energy circuits that run throughout the body. These energy circuits, or meridians as they are called, are the centerpiece of Eastern health practices and form the basis for modern-day acupuncture, acupressure, and a wide variety of other healing techniques.

This energy courses through the body and is invisible to the eye. It cannot be seen without high-tech equipment. By analogy, you do not see the energy flowing through a TV set either. You know it is there, however, by its effects. The sounds and pictures are the evidence that the energy flow exists. In the same way, EFT gives you striking evidence that energy flows within your body because it provides the effects that let you know it is there. By simply tapping near the end points of your energy meridians, you can experience some profound changes in your emotional and physical health. These changes would not occur if there was no energy system.

Western medical science tends to focus on the chemical nature of the body and, until recent years, has not paid much attention to these subtle, but powerful, energy flows. These flows do exist, however, and are attracting an expanding group of researchers. For more information, read the following:

- Becker, Robert O. *Crosscurrents*. New York: Tarcher, 1992.

- Becker, Robert O., and Gary Selden. *The Body Electric*. New York: Morrow, 1985.

- Burr, Harold S. *Blueprint for Immortality: The Electric Patterns of Life.* London: Neville Spearman, 1972.

- Nordenström, Björn. *Biologically Closed Electric Circuits: Clinical, Experimental and Theoretical Evidence for an Additional Circulatory System.* Stockholm: Nordic, 1983.

A growing number of health practitioners are finding ways to use this vital energy system to help physical healing. Acupuncturists, massage therapists, and chiropractors are but a few of them. Bookstore shelves are loaded with books on energy meridian techniques to promote physical health.

Dr. Callahan's First Experience

The science behind EFT was not developed in the way of many other discoveries. That is, it was not created in a laboratory and then tested in the real world. Instead, a stunning turn of events in the real world pointed the way first. Here's the story.

In 1980 Dr. Roger Callahan was working with a patient, Mary, for an intense water phobia. She suffered from frequent headaches and terrifying nightmares, both of which were related to her fear of water. To seek help, she had been going from therapist to therapist for years, with no material improvement.

Dr. Callahan tried to help her by conventional means for a year and a half. He didn't make much headway either. Then one day he stepped outside the normal "boundaries" of psychotherapy. Out of curiosity, he had been studying the body's energy system and decided to tap with his fingertips under her eyes (an end point of the stomach meridian). This was prompted by her complaint of some stomach discomfort.

To his astonishment, she announced immediately that her disturbing thoughts about water were gone, raced to a nearby swimming pool, and began splashing water on her face. No fear. No headaches. It all, including the nightmares, went away. And it has never returned. She is totally free of her water phobia. Results like that are rare in the field of psychotherapy, but commonplace with EFT.

The Discovery Statement

Now, with this in mind, here's the essence behind EFT: The cause of all negative emotions is a disruption in the body's energy system. I will refer to this statement henceforth as the Discovery Statement.

Let's put this in terms of Mary's water phobia. When she was experiencing her fear, the energy flowing through her stomach meridian was disrupted. That energy imbalance is what was causing her emotional intensity. Tapping under her eyes sent pulses through the meridian and fixed the disruption. It balanced it out. Once the energy meridian was balanced, the emotional intensity—the fear—went away. Therein lies the most powerful thing you are ever going to learn about your unwanted emotions: They are caused by energy disruptions.

Now let's examine the Discovery Statement in more detail. First, notice what it does not say. It does not say that a negative emotion is caused by the memory of a past traumatic experience. This is important to recognize because that presumed connection of traumatic memories to negative emotions is a mainstay in conventional psychotherapy.

In some circles, it is the accepted practice to "treat the memory" and, in the process, ask the client to relive repeatedly some emotionally painful event. EFT, by contrast, respects the memory but addresses the true cause: a disruption in the body's energy system.

People call me from all over the country for help over the telephone. Without my asking, they invariably start telling me in detail about their past traumas. That's because they mistakenly believe I need all these details to help them. To them, these memories are the cause of their problems.

The Discovery Statement
The cause of all negative emotions is a disruption in
the body's energy system.

I care deeply about helping people who needlessly carry around all these emotionally charged memories. That's why I created the course of teaching in this manual and the associated videos and audio recordings. But it always seems strange to people when I tell them they don't need to painfully relive all those horrid details for EFT to help them. These memories may contribute to an unwanted emotion (you'll see how later), but they are not the direct cause. Accordingly, we don't need to spend time painfully dwelling on them. It is superfluous to do so.

Thus there is relatively little emotional suffering involved with EFT. It is relatively painless. You will be asked to recall your problem briefly (there may be some discomfort in that), but that is all. There is no need to relive the pain. In fact, with EFT, generating prolonged emotional discomfort is frowned on. This is but one example of how EFT is a radical departure from conventional methods.

As a further aid to your learning, it might help if you again compare the energy flow in your body to that of a TV set. As long as the electricity flows through your TV normally, the sound and picture are both clear. But what would happen if you took off the back of the TV set and poked a screwdriver into all that "electronic spaghetti"? You would, quite obviously, disrupt or reroute the flow of electricity and an electric "zzzzzt" would occur inside. The picture and sound would become erratic and the TV would exhibit its version of a "negative emotion."

In the same manner, when our energy systems become imbalanced, we have an electrical "zzzzzt" effect going on inside. Straighten out this "zzzzzt" (by tapping; sometimes skillful artistry is necessary—see the recordings) and the negative emotion goes away. It's that simple. I'm well aware of how strange this may sound and how difficult it can be to believe, at least at first. I wouldn't believe it myself if I hadn't seen so many marvelous changes in people after applying these techniques.

Once you accept it, though, once you "let it in," its logic becomes undeniable. It becomes obvious and you begin to see all the weaknesses in other methods.

For example, the "treat the memory" method becomes glaringly erroneous in the light of these discoveries. It is assumed, in that method, that the past traumatic memory is the direct cause of the emotional upset in someone. It is not. There is an intermediate step, a missing piece, between the memory and the emotional upset. And that intermediate step, of course, is the disruption in the body's energy system. It is that disruption, the "zzzzzt," that is the direct cause of the emotional upset. This is portrayed in the accompanying illustration.

How a Negative Emotion is Caused

Step 1	Step 2	Step 3
	The Intermediate Step	

Distressing Memory

"zzzzzt"

A disruption in the body's energy system

Negative Emotion

Please note that if step 2, the intermediate step, does not occur, then step 3, the negative emotion, is impossible. In other words, if the memory does not cause a disruption in the body's energy system, then the negative emotion cannot occur. That is why some people are bothered by their memories and others are not. The difference is that some people's energy systems have a tendency to become imbalanced under such a memory, while others' energy systems do not.

With this in mind, it is easy to see how the "treat the memory" method misses the mark. It addresses step 1 and ignores step 2. This is why some people tend to get worse when conventional psychology aims for the memory and not its cause (the energy disruption). Addressing step 1 by requiring someone to vividly relive a distressing memory serves to induce more disruption in the energy system. And that means more pain, not less. It can, and often does, aggravate the problem. If step 2 instead of step 1 was addressed, then there would be relatively little pain. The energy system would be balanced (by appropriate tapping) and internal calm would replace the negative emotion. The result would be rapid relief because the true cause was being addressed. This happens repeatedly with EFT.

Now back again to the Discovery Statement. Please notice that it is all-inclusive. It says, "The cause of *all* negative emotions is a disruption in the body's energy system." This includes fears, phobias, anger, grief, anxiety, depression, traumatic memories, PTSD, worry, guilt, and all limiting emotions. That's a comprehensive list and covers just about every restrictive emotion we can experience. Differently stated, this means that all these negative emotions have the same cause: an electrical "zzzzzt" in the body. It also means that they can all be relieved in a similar manner.

Thus grief has the same basic cause as trauma, guilt, fear, and a baseball player's batting slump. So the same general method can be used for all these problems. This "one cause" idea is also a blessing for mental health professionals. They are accustomed to an endless, ever-changing number of explanations for the seemingly countless emotional concerns of their clients. To learn that there is only one cause greatly simplifies their efforts.

Is it possible to diagnose energy imbalances? Yes, the existence of any energy imbalance can be detected using some unique muscle-testing diagnostic techniques. Anyone skilled in these techniques can discern which energy meridian (it may be more than one) is out of balance and so know precisely where to tap to correct the imbalance—at least that's the theory. Muscle testing requires a great deal of practice, however, and few become skillful at it.

The good news is that you don't have to know anything about diagnosis to have success with EFT. This is my contribution to energy tapping procedures. EFT creates an effective end run around diagnosis. (This is not to say that the ability to diagnose is unimportant. In fact, I teach an elegant version of diagnosis in our DVD set EFT—Beyond the Basics (formerly "Steps Toward Becoming the Ultimate Therapist"). Professional therapists, especially those dealing with clinically disturbed patients, will want to go this extra step.) EFT's end run, the "100% Overhaul Concept," works admirably as a substitute for diagnosis. With this technique, diagnosis is not necessary for the majority of issues in the majority of people.

The 100% Overhaul Concept

To understand how this end run works, let's go back to the TV set analogy. Suppose your TV picture is fuzzy—there is a "zzzzzt" somewhere inside—and you want it repaired. Now suppose further that your TV repairman has no tools with which to diagnose the problem. He has no way of telling whether you need something major like a new picture tube or something minor like a new capacitor. How then does he repair your TV?

Here's the answer: He overhauls the whole thing, just as an auto mechanic might overhaul an entire engine. He replaces every electronic gizmo in sight: the picture tube, the resistors, all the wires, every capacitor, and so on. Is he overdoing it a bit? Sure! But the important question is: "Is he likely to fix the problem?" Again, sure! In fact, since he is replacing everything, his odds approach 100 percent.

Of course, the overhaul will be of limited help if the TV is located in a poor reception area where interference is present. But that's usually not the case. By the same token, a few people (less than 5 percent) have energy systems that are subject to substantial interference by allergic type reactions. We will discuss that topic later.

The 100% Overhaul Concept is EFT's end run around diagnosis. We overdo it. We use a memorized process called the Basic Recipe with which we apply enough tapping procedures to overhaul the whole energy system. This way, our odds of fixing the specific energy imbalance, or "zzzzzt," are greatly enhanced, even though we have no ability to diagnose. The difference between the TV repairman and EFT is that our overhaul takes only a few minutes, not days. Therefore it is very practical.

The 100% Overhaul Concept requires that you tap near the end points of numerous energy meridians without knowing which of them may be disrupted. In this way you "overtap" and will, in the process, tap on some energy meridians that are flowing normally. You might wonder if this does any harm. The answer is no. Thus "overtapping," as EFT requires, has the same effect as overhauling a TV set. No harm done, and you'll probably fix what's wrong.

The 100% Overhaul Concept requires a memorized tapping procedure, which is the centerpiece of EFT and is referred to as the Basic Recipe. It is your primary tool and "best friend" for emotional freedom. You now have the necessary background to appreciate its power.

Note: Please recall that the emotional and energetic releases brought about by EFT frequently result in profound physical healings.

The
Basic Recipe

Like Baking a Cake — Ingredient #1: The Setup —
Ingredient #2: The Sequence — Ingredient #3: 9 Gamut
Procedure — Ingredient #4: The Sequence (Again) — The
Reminder Phrase — Subsequent Round Adjustments

Like Baking a Cake

The goal of this manual is to equip you with an easy to use recipe for expanding your emotional freedom. I call it the Basic Recipe.

A recipe, of course, has certain ingredients that must be added in a certain order. If you are baking a cake, for example, you must use sugar instead of pepper and you must add the sugar before you put it in the oven. Otherwise, no cake.

The Basic Recipe is no exception. Each ingredient must be introduced in the proper order and must be dealt with precisely as described. Otherwise, no result.

Although I am going to some length to describe it in detail, the Basic Recipe is simple and easy to do. Once memorized, each round of it can be performed in about one minute. It will take some practice, of course, but after a few tries the whole process becomes familiar and you can bake that emotional freedom cake in your sleep. You will then be well on your way to mastery of EFT and all the rewards it provides.

Let me interject here that various shortcuts are available and described in Part II of this manual. I am describing the full Basic Recipe here because it provides an important foundation to the whole process. The proficient practitioner may want to use the shortcuts, however, because they cut the average time involved by at least half.

The full Basic Recipe consists of four ingredients, two of which are identical, as follows:

- The Setup
- The Sequence
- The 9 Gamut Procedure
- The Sequence

Ingredient #1: The Setup

Applying the Basic Recipe is something like going bowling. In bowling, there is a machine that sets up the pins by picking them up and arranging them in perfect order at the end of the alley. Once this setup is done, all you need to do is roll the ball down the alley to knock over the pins.

In a similar manner, the Basic Recipe has a beginning routine to "set up" your energy system as though it were a set of bowling pins. This routine, called the Setup, is vital to the whole process and prepares the energy system so that the rest of the Basic Recipe (the ball) can do its job.

Your energy system, of course, is not a set of bowling pins. It is a set of subtle electric circuits. I present this bowling analogy only to give you a sense of the purpose of the Setup and the need to make sure your energy system is properly oriented before attempting to remove its disruptions.

Your energy system is subject to a form of electrical interference that can block the balancing effect of these tapping procedures. When present, this interfering blockage must be removed or the Basic Recipe will not work. Removing it is the job of the Setup. Technically speaking, this interfering blockage takes the form of a polarity reversal within your energy system. This is not the same thing as the energy disruptions that cause your negative emotions.

Another analogy may help here. Consider a flashlight or any other device that runs on batteries. If the batteries aren't there, it won't work. Equally important, the batteries must be installed properly. Batteries have + and − marks on them. Those marks indicate their polarity. If you line up those + and − marks according to the instructions, then the electricity flows normally and your flashlight works fine.

But what happens if you put the batteries in backward? The flashlight will not work. It acts as if the batteries have been removed. That's what happens when polarity reversal is present in your energy system. It's like your batteries are in backward. I don't mean you stop working altogether, as in turn "toes up" and die, but your progress becomes arrested in some areas.

This polarity reversal has an official name. It is called Psychological Reversal and represents a fascinating discovery with wide-ranging application in all areas of healing and personal performance. Psychological Reversal is the reason why some diseases are chronic and respond poorly to conventional treatments. It is also the reason why some people have such a difficult time losing weight or giving up addictive substances. It is, quite literally, the cause of self-sabotage. I cover it in detail in Part II of this manual. An entire course could be dedicated to its uses, however.

For now, we need only know some foundational facts about Psychological Reversal that apply to EFT and, more important, how to correct it.

Psychological Reversal is caused by self-defeating, negative thinking, which often occurs subconsciously and thus outside of your awareness. On average, it is present, and thus hinders EFT, about 40 percent of the time. Some people have very little of it (this is rare), whereas others are beset by it most of the time (this also is rare). Most people fall somewhere in between these two extremes. Psychological Reversal doesn't create any feelings within you, so you won't know if it is present. Even the most positive people (including yours truly) are subject to it.

When it is present, it stops any attempt at healing, including EFT, dead in its tracks. Therefore it must be corrected for the rest of EFT's Basic Recipe to work.

Being true to the 100% Overhaul Concept, we correct for Psychological Reversal even though it might not be present. Correction only takes eight or ten seconds, and if it isn't present, no harm is done. If it is present, however, a major impediment to your success will be out of the way.

That being said, here's how the Setup works. There are two parts to it: (1) You repeat an affirmation three times while (2) rubbing the "Sore Spot" or, alternatively, tapping the "Karate Chop" point (these will be explained shortly).

The Affirmation. Since the cause of Psychological Reversal involves negative thinking, it should be no surprise that the correction for it includes a neutralizing affirmation. Such is the case and here it is:

Even though I have this _____, I deeply and completely accept myself.

The blank is filled in with a brief description of the problem you want to address. Here are some examples:

- Even though I have this fear of public speaking, I deeply and completely accept myself.

- Even though I have this headache, I deeply and completely accept myself.

- Even though I have this anger toward my father, I deeply and completely accept myself.

- Even though I have this war memory, I deeply and completely accept myself.

- Even though I have this stiffness in my neck, I deeply and completely accept myself.

- Even though I have these nightmares, I deeply and completely accept myself.

- Even though I have this craving for alcohol, I deeply and completely accept myself.

- Even though I have this fear of snakes, I deeply and completely accept myself.

- Even though I have this depression, I deeply and completely accept myself.

This is only a partial list, of course, because the possible issues that are addressable by EFT are endless. I apply various forms of this affirmation, including:

- I accept myself even though I have this_____.

- Even though I have this _____, I deeply and profoundly accept myself.

- I love and accept myself even though I have this _____."

All of these affirmations are correct because they follow the same general format, that is, they acknowledge the problem and create self-acceptance despite the existence of the problem. That is what's necessary for the affirmation to be effective. You can use any of them, but I suggest you use the recommended one because it is easily memorized and has a good track record in getting the job done.

Now here are some interesting points about the affirmation:

- It doesn't matter whether you believe the affirmation; just say it.

- It is better to say it with feeling and emphasis, but saying it routinely will usually do the job.

- It is best to say it out loud, but if you are in a social situation where you prefer to mutter it under your breath, or do it silently, then go ahead. It will probably be effective.

To add to the effectiveness of the affirmation, the Setup also includes the simultaneous rubbing of a "Sore Spot" or the tapping on the "Karate Chop" point. They are described next.

The Sore Spot. There are two Sore Spots and it doesn't matter which one you use. They are located in the upper left and right portions of the chest and you find them as follows: Go to the base of the throat about where a man would knot his tie. Poke around in this area and you will find a U-shaped notch at the top of your sternum (breastbone). From the top of that notch go down three inches toward your navel and over three inches to the left (or right). You should now be in the upper left (or right) portion of your chest. If you press vigorously in that area (within a two-inch radius), you will find a Sore Spot. This is the place you will need to rub while saying the affirmation.

This spot is sore when you rub it vigorously because lymphatic congestion occurs there. When you rub it, you are dispersing that congestion. Fortunately, after a few episodes the congestion is all dispersed and the soreness goes away. Then you can rub it with no discomfort whatsoever.

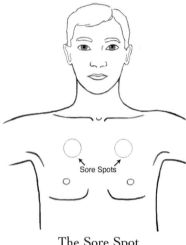

The Sore Spot

I don't mean to overplay the soreness you may feel. It's not as though you will have massive, intense pain by rubbing this Sore Spot. It is certainly bearable and should cause no undue discomfort. If it does, then lighten your pressure a little. Also, if you've had some kind of operation in that area of the chest or if there's any medical reason whatsoever why you shouldn't be probing around in that specific area, then switch to the other side. Both sides are equally effective. In any case, if there is any doubt, consult your health practitioner before proceeding, or tap the Karate Chop point instead.

The Karate Chop Point (KC). This point is located at the center of the fleshy part of the outside of your hand (either hand) between the top of the wrist and the base of the baby finger or, stated differently, the part of your hand you would use to deliver a karate chop.

The KC Point

Instead of rubbing it as you would the Sore Spot, you vigorously tap the Karate Chop point with the fingertips of the index finger and middle finger of the other hand. While you could use the Karate Chop point of either hand, it is usually most convenient to tap the Karate Chop point of the nondominant hand with the two fingertips of the dominant hand. If you are right-handed, for example, you would tap the Karate Chop point on the left hand with the fingertips of the right hand.

Should you use the Sore Spot or the Karate Chop point? After years of experience with both methods, it has been determined that rubbing the Sore Spot is a bit more effective than tapping the Karate Chop point. It doesn't have a commanding lead but it is preferred.

Because the Setup is so important in clearing the way for the rest of the Basic Recipe to work, I urge you to use the Sore Spot rather than the Karate Chop point. It puts the odds a little more in your favor. The Karate Chop point is perfectly useful, however, and will clear out any interfering blockage in the vast majority of cases. So feel free to use it if the Sore Spot is inappropriate for any reason. If you watch the videos associated with this manual (see appendix C), you will notice that I often instruct people to tap the Karate Chop point instead of rub the Sore Spot. That's because it is easier to teach when I'm on stage.

Now that you understand the parts to the Setup, performing it is easy. You create a word or short phrase to fill in the blank in the affirmation and then simply repeat the affirmation, with emphasis, three times while continuously rubbing the Sore Spot or tapping the Karate Chop point.

That's it. After a few practice rounds, you should be able to perform the Setup in eight seconds or so. Now, with the Setup properly performed, you are ready for the next ingredient in the Basic Recipe.

Ingredient #2: The Sequence

The Sequence is very simple in concept. It involves tapping on the end points of the major energy meridians in the body and is the method by which the "zzzzzt" in the energy system is balanced out. Before locating these points, however, you need a few tips on how to carry out the tapping process:

- You can tap with either hand, but it is usually more convenient to do so with your dominant hand (e.g., right hand if you are right-handed).

- Tap with the fingertips of your index finger and middle finger. This covers a little larger area than just

tapping with one fingertip and allows you to cover the
tapping points more easily.

- Tap solidly but never so hard as to hurt or bruise
  yourself.

- Tap about seven times on each of the tapping points. I
  say about seven times because you will be repeating a
  "reminder phrase" (covered later) while tapping and
  it will be difficult to count at the same time. If you tap
  a little over or a little under seven times (five to nine),
  that will be sufficient.

- Most of the tapping points exist on either side of the
  body. It doesn't matter which side you use, nor does
  it matter if you switch sides during the Sequence. For
  example, you can tap under your right eye and, later
  in the Sequence, tap under your left arm.

The Points. Each energy meridian has two end
points. For the purposes of the Basic Recipe, you need
only tap on one end to balance out any disruptions that
might exist in it. These end points are near the surface of
the body and are thus more readily accessed than other
points along the meridians that may be more deeply bur-
ied. What follows are instructions on how to locate the
end points of those meridians that are important to the
Basic Recipe. Taken together, and tapped in the order
presented, they form the Sequence.

1. At the beginning of the eyebrow, just above and to
   one side of the nose. This point is abbreviated EB for
   beginning of the EyeBrow.

2. On the bone bordering the outside corner of the eye. This point is abbreviated SE for Side of the Eye.

3. On the bone under an eye about one inch below your pupil. This point is abbreviated UE for Under the Eye.

4. On the small area between the bottom of your nose and the top of your upper lip. This point is abbreviated UN for Under the Nose.

5. Midway between the point of your chin and the bottom of your lower lip. Even though it is not directly on the point of the chin, we call it the chin point because it is descriptive enough for people to understand easily. This point is abbreviated Ch for Chin.

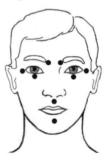

ED, SE, UE, UN and CH Points

6. The junction where the sternum (breastbone), collarbone, and the first rib meet. To locate it, first place your forefinger on the U-shaped notch at the top of the breastbone (about where a man would knot his tie). From the bottom of the U, move your forefinger

down toward the navel one inch and then to the left (or right) one inch. This point is abbreviated CB for CollarBone even though it is not on the collarbone (or clavicle) per se. It is at the beginning of the collarbone and we call it the collarbone point because that is a lot easier to say than "the junction where the sternum (breastbone), collarbone, and the first rib meet."

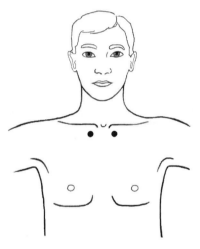

The CB Points

7. On the side of the body, at a point even with the nipple (for men) or in the middle of the bra strap (for women). It is about four inches below the armpit. This point is abbreviated UA for Under the Arm.

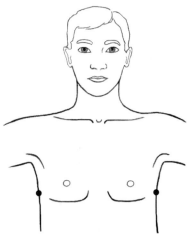

The UA Points

8. For men, one inch below the nipple. For women, where the under skin of the breast meets the chest wall. This point is abbreviated BN for Below Nipple. As discussed below, this point has been added for this edition.

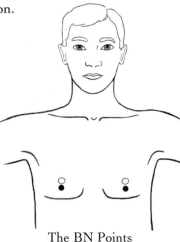

The BN Points

9. On the outside edge of your thumb at a point even with the base of the thumbnail. This point is abbreviated Th for Thumb.

The Th Point

10. On the side of your index finger (the side facing your thumb) at a point even with the base of the fingernail. This point is abbreviated IF for Index Finger.

The IF Point

11. On the side of your middle finger (the side closest to your thumb) at a point even with the base of the fingernail. This point is abbreviated MF for Middle Finger.

The MF Point

12. On the inside of your baby finger (the side clos-
    est to your thumb) at a point even with the base of
    the fingernail. This point is abbreviated BF for
    Baby Finger.

The BF Point

13. The last point is the Karate Chop point. It is located
    in the middle of the fleshy part on the outside of
    the hand between the top of the wrist bone and the
    base of the baby finger. It is abbreviated KC for
    Karate Chop.

The KC Point

Points of the Sequence

1. EB = Beginning of the EyeBrow
2. SE = Side of the Eye
3. UE = Under the Eye
4. UN = Under the Nose
5. Ch = Chin
6. CB = Beginning of the CollarBone
7. UA = Under the Arm
8. BN = Below the Nipple
9. Th = Thumb
10. IF = Index Finger
11. MF = Middle Finger
12. BF = Baby Finger
13. KC = Karate Chop

Notice that these tapping points proceed down the body, that is, each tapping point is below the one before it. That makes it a snap to memorize. A few trips through it and it should be yours forever.

Also note that the BN point has been added since the making of the videos that supplement this manual, so if you watch those, you won't see it as part of the tapping sequence. It was originally left out because it was awkward for women to tap while in social situations (such as in a restaurant). Even though the EFT results have been superb without it, I include it here for the sake of completeness.

Ingredient #3: The 9 Gamut Procedure

The 9 Gamut Procedure is, perhaps, the most bizarre-looking process in EFT. Its purpose is to "fine-tune" the brain and it does so via some eye movements, humming, and counting. Through connecting nerves, certain parts of the brain are stimulated when the eyes are moved. Likewise the right side of the brain (the creative side) is engaged when you hum a song and the left side (the digital side) is engaged when you count.

The 9 Gamut Procedure is a ten-second process wherein nine of these brain-stimulating actions are performed while continuously tapping on one of the body's energy points, the Gamut point. It has been found, after years of experience, that this routine can add efficiency to EFT and hasten progress toward emotional freedom, especially when sandwiched between two trips through the Sequence.

One way to help memorize the Basic Recipe is to use a ham sandwich analogy. The Setup is the preparation for making the ham sandwich. The sandwich itself consists of two slices of bread (the Sequence) and the ham or middle portion (the 9 Gamut Procedure).

To do the 9 Gamut Procedure, you must first locate the Gamut point. It is on the back of either hand, a half-inch toward the wrist from the point between the knuckles at the base of the ring finger and the little finger. If you draw an imaginary line between the knuckles at the base of the ring finger and little finger and consider that line to be the base of an equilateral triangle whose other sides converge to a point (apex) in the direction of the wrist, then the Gamut point would be located at the apex of the triangle.

The Gamut Point

Next, you must perform the following nine actions while tapping the Gamut point continuously:

1. Eyes closed.

2. Eyes open.

3. Eyes hard down right while holding the head steady.

4. Eyes hard down left while holding the head steady.

5. Roll eyes in a circle as though your nose was at the center of a clock and you were trying to see all the numbers in order.

6. Same as #5 only reverse the direction in which you roll your eyes.

7. Hum two seconds of a song (suggested: "Happy Birthday").

8. Count rapidly from 1 to 5.

9. Hum two seconds of a song again.

Note that these nine actions are presented in a certain order. I suggest that you memorize them in the order given. You can mix the order up if you wish, however, as long as you do all nine of them and perform 7, 8, and 9 as a unit. That is, you hum two seconds of a song, then count, then hum the song again, in that order. Years of experience have proven this to be important.

Note also that for some people humming "Happy Birthday" causes resistance because it brings up memories of unhappy birthdays. In this case, you can either use EFT on those unhappy memories and resolve them or side-step this issue for now by humming some other song.

Ingredient #4: The Sequence (Again)

The fourth, and last, ingredient in the Basic Recipe is an identical trip through the Sequence.

The Reminder Phrase

Once memorized, the Basic Recipe becomes a lifetime friend. It can be applied to an almost endless list of emotional and physical problems and provides relief from most of them. However, there's one more concept you need to understand before you can apply the Basic Recipe to a given problem. It's called the Reminder Phrase.

When a football quarterback throws a pass, he aims it at a particular receiver. He doesn't just throw the ball in the air and hope someone will catch it. Likewise, the Basic Recipe needs to be aimed at a specific problem. Otherwise, it will bounce around aimlessly with little or no effect. You "aim" the Basic Recipe by applying it while tuned in to the problem from which you want relief. This tells your system which problem needs to be the receiver.

Remember the Discovery Statement, which states: The cause of all negative emotions is a disruption in the body's energy system. Negative emotions come about because you are tuned in to certain thoughts or circumstances that, in turn, cause your energy system to disrupt. Otherwise, you function normally. A fear of heights is not present, for example, while the person is reading the comics section of the Sunday newspaper (and therefore not tuned in to the problem).

Tuning in to a problem can be done by simply thinking about it. In fact, tuning in *means* thinking about it. Thinking about the problem will bring about the energy disruptions involved, which then, and only then, can be balanced by applying the Basic Recipe. Without tuning in to the problem, and thereby creating those energy disruptions, the Basic Recipe does nothing.

Tuning in is seemingly a simple process. You merely think about the problem while applying the Basic Recipe. That's it—at least in theory. You might find it a bit difficult to consciously think about the problem while you are tapping, humming, counting, and so on. That's why I'm introducing a Reminder Phrase that you can repeat continually while you are performing the Basic Recipe.

The Reminder Phrase is simply a word or short phrase that describes the problem and that you repeat out loud each time you tap one of the points in the Sequence. In this way you continually "remind" your system about the problem you are working on.

The best Reminder Phrase to use is usually identical to what you choose for the affirmation you use in the

Setup. For example, if you are working on a fear of public speaking, the Setup affirmation would go like this:

Even though I have this fear of public speaking, I deeply and completely accept myself.

In this affirmation, the phrase "fear of public speaking" is an ideal candidate for use as the Reminder Phrase.

I sometimes use a bit shorter version of this Reminder Phrase. I might, for example, use "public speaking fear" or just "public speaking" instead of the somewhat longer version. That's just one of the shortcuts I've grown accustomed to after years of experience with these techniques. For your purposes, however, you can simplify your life by just using the identical words for the Reminder Phrase as you use for the affirmation in the Setup. That way you minimize any possibility of error.

When I am helping people with EFT, I don't always have them repeat a Reminder Phrase. That's because I have discovered over time that simply stating the affirmation during the Setup is usually sufficient to tune in to the problem at hand. The subconscious mind usually locks on to the problem throughout the Basic Recipe, even though all the tapping, humming, counting, and so on seems to be distracting. But this is not always true and, with my extensive training and experience, I am able to recognize whether using the Reminder Phrase is necessary. As stated, it is not usually necessary, but when it is, it is *really* necessary and must be used.

What's beautiful about EFT is that you don't need to have my experience in this regard. You don't have to be able to figure out whether or not the Reminder Phrase is necessary. You can just assume it is always necessary and thereby assure yourself of always being tuned in to the problem by simply repeating the Reminder Phrase as instructed. It does no harm to repeat the Reminder Phrase when it is not necessary and will be a vital tool when it is. This is part of the 100% Overhaul Concept mentioned earlier. A number of the components in each round of the Basic Recipe may not be necessary for a given problem, but when a particular part of the Basic Recipe is necessary, it is absolutely critical. So it does no harm to include everything, even what may be unnecessary. It only takes one minute per round. This includes always repeating the Reminder Phrase each time you tap a point during the Sequence. It costs nothing to include it, not even time, because it can be repeated within the same time it takes to tap each energy point seven times.

The concept of the Reminder Phrase is easy, but just to be complete I include here a few samples:

- Headache
- Anger toward my father
- War memory
- Stiffness in my neck
- Nightmares
- Craving for alcohol
- Fear of snakes
- Depression

Subsequent Round Adjustments

Let's say you are using the Basic Recipe for some problem (e.g., fear, headache, or anger). Sometimes the problem will simply vanish after just one round; at other times, one round provides only partial relief. When only partial relief is obtained, you will need to do one or more additional rounds.

Those subsequent rounds need to be adjusted slightly for best results. Here's why: One of the main reasons the first round doesn't completely eliminate a problem is because of the reemergence of Psychological Reversal, thatinterfering blockage that the Setup is designed to correct.

This time, Psychological Reversal shows up in a somewhat different form. Instead of blocking your progress altogether, it now blocks any remaining progress. You have already made some headway but become stopped partway toward complete relief because Psychological Reversal enters in a manner that keeps you from getting any better.

Since the subconscious mind tends to be literal, the subsequent rounds of the Basic Recipe need to address the fact that you are working on the remaining problem. Accordingly, the affirmation contained within the Setup needs to be adjusted, as does the Reminder Phrase.

Here's the adjusted format for the Setup affirmation:

Even though I still *have* some *of this* _____, *I deeply and completely accept myself.*

Please note the emphasized words ("still" and "some") and how they change the thrust of the affirmation toward the remainder of the problem. It should be easy to make this adjustment and, with a little experience, you will fall into it quite naturally.

Study the adjusted affirmations below. They reflect adjustments to the original affirmations shown earlier in this section.

- Even though I still have some of this fear of public speaking, I deeply and completely accept myself.

- Even though I still have some of this headache, I deeply and completely accept myself.

- Even though I still have some of this anger toward my father, I deeply and completely accept myself.

- Even though I still have some of this war memory, I deeply and completely accept myself.

- Even though I still have some of this stiffness in my neck, I deeply and completely accept myself.

- Even though I still have some of these nightmares, I deeply and completely accept myself.

- Even though I still have some of this craving for alcohol, I deeply and completely accept myself.

- Even though I still have some of this fear of snakes, I deeply and completely accept myself.

- Even though I still have some of this depression, I deeply and completely accept myself.

The Reminder Phrase is also easily adjusted. Just put the word remaining before the previously used phrase.

Here, as examples, are adjusted versions of the previous Reminder Phrases:

- Remaining headache
- Remaining anger toward my father
- Remaining war memory
- Remaining stiffness in my neck
- Remaining nightmares
- Remaining craving for alcohol
- Remaining fear of snakes
- Remaining depression

This completes the features of the Basic Recipe. You now need two things to be effective in using it. You need to memorize it and you need a few tips on how to apply it.

Tips on
How to Apply EFT

Testing — Aspects — Persistence Pays — Be Specific
When Possible — The Generalization Effect — Try It on
Everything — EFT in a Nutshell — Quick Guide to EFT

EFT is remarkably simple to apply. Just customize
the one-minute Basic Recipe with a Setup affirmation and
Reminder Phrase that aims at your problem. Then do as
many rounds as necessary until the problem is gone.

This easy process can be used, with persistence, to
reengineer your system. It will unload the fears, anger,
grief, depression and other negative emotions that cause
you to drive through life with your brakes on. And along
the way, it may give you relief from headaches, asthma,
pain and a seemingly unending list of physical ailments.

This section adds a few tips, some useful insights that
will help you make better use of EFT. It takes you behind
the scenes and helps you build a firmer foundation for
your new skills.

Testing

During EFT, evaluate the extent of your problem by rating it on a scale of 0 to 10 (where 10 represents maximum intensity and 0 represents no intensity). This provides a benchmark against which to measure your progress. You might start at a 6, for instance, and then go to a 3, then a 1, and finally to 0 as you apply rounds of the Basic Recipe.

Intensity Meter

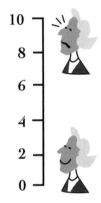

You should always measure the intensity as it exists *now* as you think about it, and not as you think it would be in the actual situation. Remember, the Basic Recipe balances the disruptions in your energy system as they exist *now* while you are tuned in to the thought or circumstance.

Here's an example of how it works. Let's say you have a fear of spiders that you would like to put behind you. If there is no spider present to cause you any emotional intensity, then close your eyes and imagine seeing a spider or imagine a past time when a spider scared you. Assess your intensity on a scale of 0 to 10 as it exists *now* while you think about it. If you estimate it at a 7, for example, then you have a benchmark against which to measure your progress.

Now do one round of the Basic Recipe and imagine the spider again. If you get no trace of your previous emotional intensity, then you are finished. If, on the other hand, you go to, let's say, a 4, then you need to perform subsequent rounds until you reach 0.

Aspects

You might wonder at this point if getting to 0 while just thinking about a spider will hold up when you are actually confronted with a real spider. The answer is usually yes! In most cases, the energy disruptions that occur while thinking about the spider are the same as those when you are in the presence of a real spider. That's why the original energy balancing tends to hold in the real circumstances.

The exception to this is when some new aspect of the problem comes up in the real situation that wasn't there when you were just thinking about it. For example, you may have been thinking about a stationary spider. If movement is an important aspect of your fear and it was absent from your thinking when the original rounds were done, then that part of the fear will arise when you see a moving spider. This is a reasonably common occurrence and it doesn't mean that EFT didn't work.

It simply means there is more to do. Just apply the Basic Recipe to the new aspect (moving spider) until your emotional response goes to 0. Once all aspects have been eliminated, your phobic response to spiders will be history and you will be perfectly calm around them.

The notion of aspects is an important one in EFT. As in the spider example, some problems have many pieces, or aspects, to them and the problem will not be completely relieved until all of these are addressed. Actually, each of these aspects qualifies as a separate problem even though they seem to be all lumped together. The fear of a stationary spider and the fear of a moving spider, for example, would seem to be lumped together. In fact, they are separate problems and need to be addressed separately by EFT.

Different aspects are possible in just about any problem you want to address with EFT. Sometimes they take the form of a series of traumatic memories such as memories of war, abuse, or rape. Each of those memories may be a separate problem, or aspect, and needs to be addressed individually before complete relief from the distress is obtained.

Please understand that where several aspects of an emotional problem are present, you may not notice any relief until all aspects are reduced to 0 by the Basic Recipe. This can be understood by comparing the process to physical healing. If, for example, you have a simultaneous headache, toothache, and stomachache, you will not feel healthy until all three are gone. The pain may seem to shift but it is, nonetheless, still pain. So it is with emotional issues that contain different aspects. Until all aspects are gone you may not feel you are getting relief, even though you have taken care of one or more aspects.

Persistence Pays

As a newcomer to EFT, you may lack the experience to be able to identify specific aspects and address them individually with the Basic Recipe. That's okay. You need only go with whatever feeling you are having and address that feeling with the Basic Recipe. Your subconscious mind knows what you are working on. You might address this "feeling" with a Setup affirmation such as "Even though I have this feeling, I deeply and completely accept myself" and a Reminder Phrase of "This feeling."

Please understand that the majority of the problems the Basic Recipe addresses are not laden with numerous aspects. Most problems are easy to identify and just as easily relieved. But just in case you happen to have one of those more involved problems and you are unable to identify specific aspects of it, I suggest you do three rounds of the Basic Recipe for "this feeling" or "this problem" once per day (that's about three minutes per day) for thirty days. Your subconscious mind has a way of bringing up what is necessary and you should have relief long before the thirty days are up. EFT, as you can tell, is a very flexible process and will often make progress on problems that are outside your awareness.

Be Specific When Possible

It is best, of course, to be specific whenever you can. That way you can efficiently zero in on an exact fear, pain, or memory and eliminate it from your limiting baggage. Sometimes people lump together a number of specific problems under a larger heading. This can handicap your progress with EFT. For example, most people would like to have a better self-image but don't realize that the term is a general label that serves as a catchall phrase for numerous specific problems (e.g., memories of abuse, rejection, failure, and/or fears of various kinds).

People who have been subject to severe rejection as children are likely to feel inadequate in many areas of life. This contributes to their poor self-image by causing energy disruptions (and hence negative emotions) when they face potential rejection. Accordingly, they consistently feel "not good enough" when given opportunities and tend to stay stuck where they are in life. When lumped together with other negative emotions, self-image problems become more widely generalized and the individuals feel stopped in even more areas.

I use an analogy to put self-image and other general emotional labels into proper EFT perspective. I liken the general problem to a diseased forest in which each of the underlying specific issues is a negative tree. The forest, at first, is so densely populated with trees that it may seem impossible to find your way out. To some, it may even seem like a jungle.

When you neutralize each specific negative event in your life with the Basic Recipe, you are, effectively, cutting down a negative tree. Continue cutting down these trees and, after a while, the forest will have thinned out so you can walk out of it rather easily. Each toppled tree represents another degree of emotional freedom, and if you are persistent with the Basic Recipe, you will gradually find your negative responses subsiding. You will find yourself calm and at ease when faced with new opportunities, and you will be guided by a new sense of adventure rather than by a fear of not being "good enough."

One very helpful concept here is to break down problems into the specific events that underlie them and use EFT on each such specific event. For example, if you have anger because your father abused you, apply EFT to specific events such as "When Dad hit me in the kitchen at age eight." This is often superior to using EFT on the more global issue of "My father abused me."

Perhaps the biggest mistake made by newcomers is that they try to use EFT on issues that are too global. They may make good headway with persistence, but are less likely to notice the results right away. As a result they may quit too soon. Break the problems down into specific events and you will notice results on those specific events right away. Doing this also addresses the true cause and is usually more efficient.

The Generalization Effect

That being said, I want to acquaint you now with a fascinating feature of EFT. I call it the Generalization Effect because, after you address a few related problems with EFT, the process starts to generalize over all those problems. For example, someone who has a hundred traumatic memories of being abused usually finds that they all vanish after using EFT to neutralize only five or ten of them. This is startling to some people because they have so many traumas in their life they think they are in for unending sessions with these techniques. Not so—at least not usually. EFT often clears out a whole forest after cutting down just a few trees.

Try It on Everything

The problems to which EFT can be applied range from the fear of public speaking to intense war memories, from chocolate cravings to insomnia, from hiccups to multiple sclerosis. I know of no limit to the emotional and physical problems that EFT can address. Accordingly, I try it on everything and urge you to do the same. People are forever asking me, "Will it work on _____?" and I always respond with "Try it!" I have given up being surprised at the results. Headway is usually gained.

This "Try it on everything" idea must be interpreted with common sense, however. Its purpose is to expand your awareness of EFT's possibilities. It is not a license to act irresponsibly. Accordingly, you should not try EFT on serious mental illnesses or anything else *unless* you are properly trained or qualified in that area.

EFT in a Nutshell

I value clarity and strive to inject it into what I teach. To me, the ultimate evidence of clarity is being able to reduce the subject matter to a simple paragraph. I have done that with EFT. Here is EFT in a nutshell:

Memorize the Basic Recipe. Aim it at any emotional or physical problem by customizing it with an appropriate Setup affirmation and Reminder Phrase. Be specific when possible and aim EFT at the specific emotional events in your life that might underlie the problem. When necessary, be persistent until all aspects of the problem have vanished. Try it on everything!

That's it. That's the essence of what you are learning here. For an expanded version of this summary, see the following, "Quick Guide to EFT." This gives you, on a single page, the Discovery Statement, the Basic Recipe, and EFT in a Nutshell. You might wish to use it as a quick reference until you master these procedures.

Quick Guide to EFT

I. The Discovery Statement

The cause of all negative emotions is a disruption in the body's energy system.

II. EFT in a Nutshell

Memorize the Basic Recipe. Aim it at any emotional or physical problem by customizing it with an appropriate Setup affirmation and Reminder Phrase. Be specific when possible and aim EFT at the specific emotional events in your life that might underlie the problem. When necessary, be persistent until all aspects of the problem have vanished. Try it on everything!

III. The Basic Recipe

1. **The Setup:** Repeat 3 times this affirmation:

   "Even though I have this _____, I deeply and completely accept myself."

   while continuously rubbing the Sore Spot or tapping the Karate Chop point.

2. **The Sequence:** Tap about 7 times on each of the following energy points while repeating the Reminder Phrase at each point.

EB, SE, UE, UN, Ch, CB, UA, BN, Th, IF, MF, BF, KC

3. **The 9 Gamut Procedure:** Continuously tap on the Gamut point while performing each of these 9 actions:

   (1) Eyes closed (2) Eyes open (3) Eyes hard down right (4) Eyes hard down left (5) Roll eyes in circle (6) Roll eyes in other direction (7) Hum 2 seconds of a song (8) Count to 5 (9) Hum 2 seconds of a song.

4. **The Sequence (again):** Tap about 7 times on each of the following energy points while repeating the Reminder Phrase at each point.

EB, SE, UE, UN, Ch, CB, UA, BN, Th, IF, MF, BF, KC

   Note: In subsequent rounds the Setup affirmation and the Reminder Phrase are adjusted to reflect the fact that you are addressing the remaining problem.

5

Frequently Asked Questions

Some people are astonished at what they see with EFT. Their questions are openly enthusiastic. Others don't quite know how to respond because EFT violates most of their beliefs about personal improvement. Their questions contain an element of caution, as though they are semi-open but still need to protect their existing beliefs. Whatever their source, these questions are important to your education in EFT because they help fill in gaps you might have in your understanding. For this purpose, I include here the standard questions I have received over the years and my answers.

Q. How do EFT results differ from a quick fix?

A. The label "quick fix" carries with it a negative connotation and is often used to label the questionable healing techniques of hucksters and cheats. The term goes hand in hand with the term "con man" and, when used, often brings about thoughts of suspicion and caution.

EFT offers rapid relief from numerous emotional and physical ailments without meriting the negative label "quick fix." This is obvious to those who review the case histories detailed here and in the videos and audio recordings (see appendix C) and is even more obvious to students who have experienced the results firsthand. I use the term "rapid relief" instead of "quick fix" to put across the same idea but without the negative connotation.

Now here's an important note: Throughout history, healing techniques of various kinds have usually been slow and inefficient until someone finds the true remedy for the ailment. When the true remedy is found, everything changes and the old methods become relics of the past. Polio is a case in point. Until the Salk vaccine was discovered, poliomyelitis was considered incurable and all manners of medications and therapies (including the iron lung) were employed to help the sufferers. They didn't do much, of course. They helped ease some of the discomfort and limited some of the long-term damage caused by the disease, but that was about it. And then came the Salk vaccine. It did away with all the antiquated, inefficient attempts at alleviating polio and replaced them with a true remedy. It was, indeed, a quick fix—without the negative connotation.

The eradication of polio is only one example wherein inefficient methods gave way to true remedies.

Penicillin was another "quick fix" miracle drug that provided instant cures for illnesses ranging from respiratory diseases to gonorrhea. More examples abound, but the point is that procedures such as EFT are replacing all the inefficient techniques aimed at improving emotional health. The fact that these procedures give rapid relief to seemingly difficult emotional problems is impressive evidence that they represent the true remedy. If they took forever to do very little, then they would have simply taken their place among the other ho-hum techniques of the past. But they don't. They hit the bull's-eye and perform as a true remedy should: quickly, easily, and permanently.

Q. Does it last?

A. This question is usually a companion to the "quick fix" question. After all, the "logic" goes, any solution that can be achieved that fast must be temporary. Lasting results, at least in the minds of most people, must take time to produce.

Not so. EFT's results are usually permanent. The case histories in this manual feature just a few of the people who have had lasting results even though the problem was relieved in moments. This is still more evidence that EFT is addressing the true cause of the problem. Otherwise, the remedy would not be so long lasting.

Please remember, however, that EFT doesn't do everything for everyone. Some problems seem to reappear. This is usually caused by different aspects of the original problem showing up at a later time. The experienced student of EFT will recognize this and simply reapply the Basic Recipe for this new aspect. The experienced student will also break the problem down into specific events and apply EFT to those underlying causes. In time, after all aspects and specific events have been addressed, the problem usually goes away completely and does not return.

Q. How does EFT handle emotional problems that are very intense and/or have been with a person for a very long time?

A. The same way it handles every other emotional problem. In EFT, the intensity of a problem or how long it has been around is immaterial. The cause is always a disrupted energy system and using the Basic Recipe to balance it gives relief, regardless of the severity of the problem.

This question usually arises from the belief that intense and/or long-term problems are more "deeply ingrained" than other problems. Therefore it should take more effort to relieve them. This seems logical when viewed through a conventional mindset because conventional approaches don't directly address the true cause.

Conventional approaches tend to take aim at one's memories or other mental processes and ignore the energy system (where the true cause lies). When progress is slow, it is convenient to blame the problem because it is presumed to be "deeply ingrained" or otherwise difficult to deal with. In this manner, conventional approaches can, and do, explain away ineffectiveness.

When EFT requires persistence, it is *not* because of the intensity or resident length of a problem. It is usually because of a problem's complexity. Complexity, in EFT, means the existence of several aspects to a problem, each of which must be relieved before total relief is felt. The notion of aspects is covered repeatedly in this manual.

Note: These comments may or may not apply to serious mental illness. The application of EFT to such disorders has proven helpful, but only a professional skilled in this area should use EFT in this way.

Q. How does EFT deal with the need to understand one's problem?

A. This is one of the most astonishing features about EFT. A shift in people's understanding of their problem happens simultaneously with the relief. After EFT, people talk about their problem differently. They put it in a healthy perspective. The typical rape victim, for example, no longer carries a deep fear and distrust of men. Rather, she considers her assailant(s) to have the problem and in need of help.

People who use EFT for relief from guilt no longer take blame for whatever event gave rise to the guilt. Anger turns to objectivity. Grief turns to a healthy, more peaceful perspective about the death of a loved one.

Notice how you and others respond to your former problem and you will see what I mean. Your understanding shifts right along with the relief.

Here's a final note on how powerfully EFT shifts understanding. Of the hundreds and hundreds of people my colleague Adrienne Fowlie and I have helped with EFT, not one of them has ever asked to better understand their problem. Why would they? There was no need.

Q. How does EFT deal with stress and anxiety?

A. In EFT, stress and anxiety have the same cause as all other negative emotions: a disruption in the body's energy system. Accordingly, they are addressed with the Basic Recipe, the same as any other emotional issue.

Anxiety has a specific meaning in clinical psychology. It refers to an intense fear or dread lacking an unambiguous cause or a specific threat. In EFT, however, we give it a much broader definition to include that general state of uneasiness that is more commonly known as anxiety. Under that definition, stress and anxiety fall into the same category. Stress and anxiety tend to be ongoing problems because the circumstances that create them are ongoing. An abusive family situation and a stressful job environment are but two of a long list of possibilities. EFT does not do away with the circumstances, of course, but it is an important aid in reducing your anxious responses. In most cases, EFT will need to be used persistently (most likely daily) because the stressful circumstances tend to show up every day.

After a while, you should notice that your responses to difficult events are much calmer. Things just don't get to you like they used to. You smile more. Your health improves and life seems easier.

Q. How does EFT help with sports performance?

A. Ask any accomplished athlete and they will tell you emphatically that their mental state is critical to their performance. The difference between good days and bad days for the athlete is almost always due to emotional causes. Barring sickness, the athlete always brings the same highly skilled body into the field of battle. The only thing that changes is the effect that emotions have on the body.

Most people, and athletes are no exception, have their share of negative thoughts and self-doubt. By now you are quite familiar with the fact that those negative states of mind disrupt the body's energy system and cause negative emotions. These negative emotions show up in the body in a variety of ways (e.g., pounding heart, tears, sweating) and this includes some tension in the muscles.

In athletics, timing is everything and even the slightest tension in the muscles affects it. Hitting a baseball, tennis ball or golf ball requires perfect timing and being off by just an eighth of an inch is the difference between hitting a home run and a fly ball, between acing a tennis serve and sending the ball into the net, or between sinking or missing a putt. Athletes are well aware of this problem and many hire sports psychologists to help them deal with it. Any negative emotion, even the mild ones and the subconscious ones, can critically affect an athlete's performance.

EFT provides a remarkably effective solution to this problem. The purpose of the Basic Recipe is to neutralize negative emotions and their effects. One of the most common responses to it is that people feel relaxed, which is another way of saying that tension has left their muscles. This is ideal for the athlete because it neutralizes unnecessary emotional tension in the muscles, without affecting their athletic ability. It allows their potential to flow through without being hindered by any resistance in the muscles.

Q. Why does EFT give surprisingly good relief from physical problems?

A. This is easy to understand in light of the increasing acceptance of the existence of the mind-body connection. EFT provides striking evidence of this connection. What more obvious proof could one want than to watch changes in both mind and body occur as a result of tapping on the body's energy system?

But the evidence goes even deeper than this. Applying EFT to emotional issues often brings on the cessation of physical problems. Breathing problems go away. Headaches vanish. Joint pains subside. Multiple sclerosis symptoms improve. I have witnessed this phenomenon for years. The list of physical improvements brought about by EFT is endless.

The logical inference from this is that EFT effectively addresses any emotional contributors to physical symptoms. Once the emotional contributors are out of the way, the symptoms subside.

There are those, of course, who believe that emotions or mental processes are the only cause of physical diseases. I don't know how to prove or disprove that notion but I offer here the rather obvious fact that emotions, at the very least, substantially contribute to physical health. And EFT is an efficient tool for relief in this regard.

One final note on this: You might wonder what is happening "behind the emotional scenes" when you apply the Basic Recipe directly to a physical symptom (such as a headache) without zeroing in on a specific emotion. Stated differently, if the physical symptom is caused by some emotional issue, then why is there relief of the physical symptom when no specific emotion was addressed? I don't know for sure. There is much to learn about these techniques, and the future, I'm sure, will bring us some exciting revelations on many fronts. For now, I believe that the subconscious mind brings up whatever emotional issue is contributing to the cause of the physical symptom. Applying the Basic Recipe automatically addresses that emotion.

Q. How can I keep up to date with the latest advances in EFT?

A. Although you can generate impressive results just with what you learn in this manual, you must recognize that this is only a beginning. EFT is capable of far more than what you learn here. Here are three resources:

- www.emofree.com/products.htm for a list of advanced video products

- www.emofree.com/tutorial.htm for a description of some of the latest techniques and findings

- www.emofree.com/faq.htm for frequently asked questions

6

Case Histories

Fear of Public Speaking — Asthma — Sexual Abuse —
Anxiety and Fingernail Biting — Fear of Spiders — Coffee
Addiction — Alcoholism — Grief — Fear of Needles —
Addiction to Peanut M&M's — Physical Pain — Low
Back Pain — Guilt and Insomnia — Constipation — Body
Embarrassment — Lupus — Ulcerative Colitis — Panic
Attack — Fear of Elevators

What follows are examples of actual results with
EFT. They demonstrate EFT in action on a wide variety
of problems and give you a sense of what to expect. Please
read them all, even if some do not appear to apply to you.
There is a lot of overlap in how these techniques work and
what applies to one problem can also apply in another.

Further, an important part of your EFT education is
to recognize the various approaches that can be used on
a wide variety of ailments. EFT applies to almost every

emotional and physical ailment known to humankind and the procedure itself is basically the same for each ailment. The approaches can vary widely, however. Although the following case histories give you some sense of the varying approaches, the videos detailed in appendix C are much more useful in this regard. We are limited in what we can do on the printed page.

Case History #1: Fear of Public Speaking

Sue had a speech impediment that resulted in an advanced fear of public speaking. She attended one of our workshops and asked my colleague Adrienne and me for some help during the lunch break. She showed us a scar on her neck where an operation for throat cancer had been performed. As a result of her operation, she could not speak normally and it was difficult to understand her. She was understandably terrified of public speaking and, to make matters worse, she was a sergeant in the army and had to "public speak" frequently in front of her troops.

We applied two rounds of the Basic Recipe and she overcame the fear in a few minutes—at least while thinking about it. When the workshop reconvened, I asked her to come up on stage to test her fear of public speaking. As she walked toward the stage, she reported that her fear was upon her again, but it was "only a 3," she said. This was much less than the 10 she usually felt, but, obviously, there was still some left. This is prime evidence that some new aspect of her fear was emerging that wasn't present in her thinking during the break.

We applied one more round of the Basic Recipe on stage (while she faced the audience) and the fear fell to zero. She then grabbed my microphone, asked me to sit down and enchanted this audience of a hundred people as she told the story of what happened over the break. She was filled with calm and poise. The speech impediment was still there, of course, but the fear was gone.

Does eliminating the fear of public speaking make someone a great speaker? No, of course not. Public speaking is an art and takes practice to perfect. What it does do, though, is remove the pounding heart, dry mouth, and other fear symptoms so that one is free and comfortable in developing public speaking skills.

Case History #2: Asthma

Kelly sat in the front row at one of my presentations. Her asthma was obvious, as I could hear her labored breathing throughout my talk. It was severe enough to sound something like a mild snore and clearly annoyed some of the people near her.

After the presentation, she asked me to help her with her fear of public speaking. Interestingly, she did not "get" that EFT could relieve asthma so she didn't ask for help on this obvious problem. To her, nothing but medicine could help.

So we addressed her fear of public speaking. About three minutes into the EFT procedures, she remarked, with a bit of astonishment in her voice, that her breathing had eased. And indeed it had. There was no sign of asthma.

We often get "bonus results" like this. Balancing the body's energy system can pay great dividends.

As of this writing, I have only addressed perhaps eight or ten problems that also involve asthma, breathing, or sinus-related problems. I have seen clear progress in each case. I mean by this that there was immediate relief every time EFT was applied. I'm not saying, however, that EFT eliminated the physical problem forever, as is often the case with emotional issues. Sometimes the breathing problem comes back and requires additional rounds of EFT.

Please understand that I apply EFT to more people than I can count and it is impractical for me to follow up on all of them. So I don't know how many need to repeat the procedures to relieve asthma symptoms. I only know that there is a high likelihood for relief. If you are an asthma sufferer, you have an excellent chance of gaining relief from your problem. Please do this with the aid of your physician, however.

Case History #3: Sexual Abuse

Bob was repeatedly subjected to sexual abuse as a youngster. His memories of it were very intense and created great anger within him. The abusive events were almost thirty years ago and he knew, logically, that retaining the anger was costing him his peace of mind. Emotionally, however, he couldn't seem to shake it.

It took two unusual sessions to give him relief on this issue. I say unusual because it was done in a workshop environment in front of other people. Understandably, he didn't want to discuss the sexual abuse with others, so I helped him apply EFT to the memories in a way that maintained his privacy.

This is easily done with EFT because all that is required is that the client "tune in" to the problem while performing the tapping techniques. The "tuning in" can be done privately.

I ran into Bob about a month later and he said he "didn't think about it much any more." This is a typical response after using EFT. Even the most intense issues tend to fade away. Sometimes people report that, after EFT, they can't even recall the memory. That is inaccurate, although it can seem that way. The memory doesn't really go away because when I ask them to describe it, they can still do so in great detail. What happens is the emotional sting vanishes and thus the memory doesn't come up in the same way. It is now a mild event from the past. It just seems like they can no longer recall it because it is missing a previously powerful ingredient. This is what you want, of course. We are looking for emotional freedom here, not amnesia.

EFT was not 100 percent successful in this case, however, because Bob still had occasional, relatively mild, bouts with the memories. But it's nothing like it was. He can probably eliminate it completely over time if he persistently uses these techniques.

Case History #4: Anxiety and Fingernail Biting

Susan had an ongoing level of anxiety and chose to do EFT frequently throughout the day. She did this for several months and, as her anxiety level subsided, she quit biting her fingernails (a lifelong habit), without even trying. She picked up her guitar one day and noticed that her fingernails were too long to play it.

EFT sometimes works in subtle ways and positive side effects like this often happen outside your awareness. When your life returns to normal in some area (as in the reduction of anxiety), it seems well...uh...normal. There are no bells and whistles, just relative peace. Often you don't even notice the change until someone brings it to your attention.

That's what happened with Susan and her fingernails. EFT subtly, but powerfully, reduced her anxiety to the point where biting her fingernails was no longer necessary.

Case History #5: Fear of Spiders

Molly felt intense emotion when just thinking about spiders and had nightmares about them five nights a week. She got completely over her fear in just two sessions with EFT.

In the first session, Adrienne used EFT to reduce Molly's fear to zero while she was just thinking about spiders. Often this is enough and the fear stays at zero even when confronted with a real spider.

But to make sure, Adrienne took Molly to a pet store to see a tarantula. Molly, once again, became very fearful and ran crying out of the pet store. This was not the fault of the first round of EFT. Rather, it was an indication that the real spider brought up new aspects of the fear that weren't present when just the thought was going on.

After a few more minutes with EFT, Molly went back into the pet store and calmly viewed the tarantula. The fear was gone.

A few days later, Molly called Adrienne to report that she was at the house of a girlfriend who owned a pet tarantula (a variety harmless to humans). She said they took the spider out of the cage and Molly let it crawl on her.

Here is a classic example of the power of these techniques. Even people without a noticeable fear of spiders would not let a tarantula, even the harmless kind, crawl on them. But Molly was perfectly relaxed about it and had less fear than the normal everyday citizen. Please note, however, that EFT does not make people stupid. Molly would not have let the spider crawl on her if it was, indeed, dangerous. EFT removes the irrational portion of phobic fears but does not reduce normal caution.

Months later, we spoke with Molly and the fear still had not returned. In addition, she no longer had nightmares about spiders.

Case History #6: Coffee Addiction

Joe had quit drinking coffee but still craved it. He attended one of my workshops and observed me applying EFT to someone else who wanted to get over their craving for coffee. He tapped along with us, although he did it in the background, and his coffee cravings went away—permanently. In this case, EFT broke the addiction in one application.

Just so you know, that doesn't usually happen. EFT is a marvelous tool for getting over immediate cravings and is thus a major help in relieving withdrawal symptoms. But it usually requires many repeated applications before the addiction disappears. About 5 percent of the people have Joe's response. The rest take longer.

Along these same lines, however, Susan, a psychotherapist, got over an addiction to soft drinks in one two-minute session and Robb did the same thing for chocolate.

Case History #7: Alcoholism

Aaron got over his addiction to alcohol. This, of course, is a much more serious addiction than coffee, soft drinks, or chocolate. He went to bed drunk every night and spent his days with a hangover. In his words, "Alcohol was my God."

We needed several sessions with EFT and he performed the routines several times per day. As a result, withdrawal was easy.

In the early stages of his recovery, he walked by his formerly favorite beer at the supermarket with a sense of pride. And now, one year later, he finds it repulsive. He has no cravings for alcohol whatsoever. He has his life back. He even passed up a New Year's Eve party because he "didn't want to be around a bunch of drunks."

Here's a note of common sense. Once an addiction is broken, that doesn't mean you can't become re-addicted. Once you get over your addiction to alcohol, or anything else, stay away from it or you will need to break the addiction again. EFT does not allow you to "have a little now and then" of your addictive substance.

Case History #8: Grief

Alicia carried such grief over the death of her brother that, even after two years, she still couldn't speak about it. Her emotions were too intense to get the words out.

I was asked to give a workshop at a convention she was attending and was allowed to apply these techniques to a handful of volunteers the night before the presentation. Alicia volunteered and we worked on her grief in a fifteen-minute session that included seven other people.

The next morning, midway through the workshop, she voluntarily stood up in front of eighty people and expressed her amazement that she could talk calmly about her brother's death. It still wasn't her favorite subject, but the grief was gone.

By the way, everyone in that small group made progress during the fifteen-minute session. One woman got over a height phobia (she tested it several minutes later by looking over a high hotel balcony with no problem), one man got over anger at a past situation, and the others got noticeable relief from a variety of emotional issues.

Case History #9: Fear of Needles

Connie was very anxious around needles. She would become nauseous and would often faint when it was necessary to have her blood taken. This was limiting, indeed, if she was to have regular physical examinations and maintain good health. Adrienne applied EFT to her for just a few minutes. The fear went away and her next exposure to needles was without fear.

This is typical, especially with phobic responses like this. Usually, just a few minutes with the techniques create a lasting result. This is true even if the object of the phobia (needles, in this case) is not present at the time. In those few times that the actual situation still brings on some of the fear, it usually only takes another round or so of EFT to eliminate it permanently.

Case History #10: Addiction to Peanut M&M's

Nancy was facing surgery and her doctor advised her to lose weight so that the surgery would go more smoothly. Part of her challenge in losing weight was passing up Peanut M&M's. She had been addicted to them for years.

She used EFT to reduce her immediate craving and, to her surprise, had the experience of totally severing the addiction in about three minutes.

This "bonus result" happens now and then. After that, Nancy had no difficulty refraining from eating Peanut M&M's.

Addictions are linked to, and caused by, various forms of anxiety. If you address the anxiety, which is done so powerfully with EFT, then the need for the addictive substance subsides.

Case History #11: Physical Pain

Lea attended one of the workshops I did for hypnotherapy students. She told me before the workshop that she had a lot of tight muscles and physical pain. I walked her through EFT for relief of the pain in her neck and shoulders. It subsided within two minutes.

About an hour into the three-hour workshop, I asked her if the pain in her neck and shoulders had come back. She said no and then added that the rest of the pain in her body had subsided but was not completely gone.

Here's another example of how we address one problem with EFT and other healings occur along the way. In Lea's case, the relief we gave to her neck and shoulder pain spilled over to the rest of her body.

We then did another round of EFT and the balance of the pain went away, and it stayed away for the rest of the workshop.

Pain like this is often caused by emotional distress and that's why EFT can be so effective in addressing it. However, new emotional stresses may bring the pain back. If so, repeated uses of EFT will likely give relief.

Case History #12: Low Back Pain

Donna is another example along these lines. She, too, attended one of my workshops, and had such severe lower back pain that she didn't think she could stay for the whole one-day workshop. "I just can't sit that long," she said.

I helped her with EFT and her back did not bother her for the rest of the day. She stayed for the entire workshop.

Case History #13: Guilt and Insomnia

Audrey is a severely disturbed woman whom I met with at the request of her therapist. She had been abused physically, mentally, and sexually all her life and had a long list of emotional problems that were a challenge to any therapist.

I only met with Audrey for forty-five minutes. In that time I learned that she carried great guilt over the burning down of her house. It seems she fell asleep one night with a candle going. Her cat subsequently knocked over the candle, which, in turn, started the fire.

Though it may seem obvious that guilt is not in order here, that was not the case with Audrey. She couldn't speak about it without tears. She blamed herself for the entire episode.

I walked her through EFT and her guilt appeared to go away. To test it, I let about twenty minutes go by while changing the subject to other things. Then I asked her to tell me the story about her house burning down.

To the surprise of her therapist, she said, matter-of-factly, "It wasn't my fault," and went on to another subject. No tears. No emotional intensity. The guilt had simply disappeared—in minutes.

I tell you this to illustrate a point. EFT can be so powerful that the changes often feel normal. Accordingly, you may not "feel any different" when using EFT for certain problems (like guilt). But listen to what you say about it over time. You will tend to dismiss the problem and it will cease to occupy your emotional space. It will vanish without any fanfare. That is powerful, indeed, and is precisely what you want. It is the ultimate in emotional freedom.

Audrey also had a problem with insomnia. She slept very little, maybe two hours per night, and had to take drugs to do that. At the end of our session, I had her lie down on a table in her therapist's office and applied EFT to her for sleeping. Within sixty seconds she was sound asleep. I stayed to speak with the therapist for another thirty minutes and, at the end of that time, Audrey was snoring loudly. She was "gone." No drugs, no pills, nothing but tapping on a badly disrupted energy system.

Case History #14: Constipation

Richard had been constipated for twenty-five years. He was taking Metamucil twice a day and still had difficulty "being regular."

I taught him EFT for this problem and he performed the routine diligently several times per day. After two weeks, there was no noticeable improvement. I told him to be persistent and keep at it. Sometimes these things take more time.

I spoke with him two months later and things had improved significantly. He was now taking Metamucil only twice a week instead of twice a day.

As a student of EFT you must understand that sometimes persistence is important. Although emotional problems are often disposed of rapidly and the same is true of many physical problems, some situations just take longer and it isn't easy to predict which ones they are. If Richard had given up after two weeks, he would not have made this headway. The message? Hang in there.

Case History #15: Body Embarrassment

Adrienne and I met Bingo at a workshop we gave in Los Angeles. He was a body builder and had shaped himself so magnificently that fitness magazines frequently offered him several thousand dollars to pose for photographs. But Bingo often turned down these offers because he had intense emotional discomfort about revealing his body in public. He was of Asian descent and explained that, in his family, showing off the body was a shameful thing to do.

He came up on stage to try to get beyond this problem and became very nervous right away. In fact, he said, "If you make me take off my shirt, I'll kill you." Of course he didn't mean it literally, but it was certainly an indication of the intensity of his emotions about it.

After three or four minutes with EFT, he smiled and calmly took off his shirt to an enthusiastic applause from the audience. A day or two later he accepted an offer to pose for a magazine for three thousand dollars.

I don't think, however, that he got totally beyond his problem. He made some obvious progress, but when he took his shirt off he held it in his hands as though he might like to put it back on. He didn't just throw it aside. Chances are he needed a few more rounds of EFT to get rid of the problem completely.

But please remember, this was done under adverse circumstances in relation to his issue, that is, on stage. To make as much headway as we did, which I judge to be about 70 percent, is remarkable given the setting.

Case History #16: Lupus

Carolyn was my first major surprise at how well these techniques can work with physical problems. She attended one of my daylong seminars during my early years with EFT. I only spent an hour hitting the highlights of how it worked and helped a few people get over their height phobias (including Carolyn) and their immediate craving for chocolate.

What I didn't know was that Carolyn had lupus, a serious degenerative disease. I was simply too busy dealing with many people at once to notice that her hands and feet were swollen from the disease. In fact, she told me later that she couldn't wear normal shoes because of the swelling.

During the seminar I taught a shortened version of what you are learning in this manual. Carolyn decided to tap several times per day for her lupus condition and, to her surprise, all her symptoms subsided.

She came to another presentation of mine two months later and told me what had happened. The only thing she had done differently was EFT. She showed me her hands and feet and reported that the swelling had gone completely away. She also said that her energy level had risen to a point where she went dancing frequently. This is something she couldn't do before.

So does this mean EFT will cure lupus? I'm not saying that, although it is very hard to ignore what happened.

EFT obviously helped with her symptoms. I offer this stunning example as evidence of the power of EFT and encourage you to apply it even for serious diseases. But please, please do so with the supervision of your physician.

I called Carolyn several months later to see how her lupus was. She had stopped doing her daily tapping and the symptoms had begun to reappear. Sometimes physical problems go away completely with no more tapping and sometimes not. This is a case of sometimes not.

What is important to recognize here is what did happen, not what didn't. Serious symptoms definitely subsided while balancing the energy system. That is not to be dismissed.

Case History #17: Ulcerative Colitis

Here's another case of a serious disease. Dorothy had ulcerative colitis and was taking heavy medication that had many negative side effects. Ulcerative colitis is a painful disease of the colon. In Dorothy's case, it was severe. After tests, her doctors had reported, using lay terms, that her colon was "90 percent infected."

Dorothy worked with Adrienne and did two things: (1) she became a vegetarian and (2) she began using EFT daily for her disease. She began to feel much better within a few weeks and chose to slack off on her medication. (Note: we never advise people to discontinue medication without consulting their physician.)

About six months later, her doctors examined her colon again and reported it as "10 percent infected." That was three years ago and she has had little or no trouble with it since. In fact, a year ago she gave birth to a child.

Now what do you suppose caused her disease to subside? Was it the vegetarian diet or EFT, or both? There is no way to tell for sure. People often try several healing methods simultaneously and so it is hard to say which contributed the most.

Once you have more experience with EFT, you might conclude, as I have, that it should always be included as one of the healing techniques in any condition.

Case History #18: Panic Attack

Kerry, in the midst of a panic attack, called Adrienne from a Lake Tahoe hotel. If you are familiar with panic attacks, you know of the overpowering terror they bring on. People who are experiencing one often think they are going to die. Such was the case with Kerry. She called Adrienne with obvious panic in her voice and immediately gave her room number so she could be found if she became unconscious or died.

Adrienne walked her through EFT over the phone and got her over the serious part of her panic within a few minutes. By contrast, sufferers of this condition often endure this intense fear for several hours. To take the edge off within minutes is a welcome relief indeed. In Kerry's case, another twenty minutes was required to bring it way down.

Case History #19: Fear of Elevators

Ellen used EFT to eliminate her fear of elevators. She approached me during a break in one of my seminars and asked me if I could help her with this lifelong fear. She was understandably timid and cautious about her request, as are most people who suffer from intense fears. Conventional psychology often requires phobics to confront their fear head-on. Fear-laden people are typically asked to grit their teeth, clench their fist, and get on that elevator. In this way, the logic goes, the fearful person becomes "desensitized" or "gets used to" the fear. To me that's a well-meant, but unnecessary, practice, which, in comparison to EFT, creates unjustifiable pain. It often serves to scare people out of their socks and gives them yet another fearful trauma to overcome. Such practices are no longer necessary.

Since EFT is about as pain free as these things get, I told Ellen that we wouldn't go near an elevator until she felt totally comfortable about it.

So we stayed in the seminar room and spent three or four minutes applying EFT. She then said that she had never been so relaxed about elevators before and was ready to go on one.

Fortunately, we were in a hotel and were about thirty steps from an elevator. Normally, as a caution, I would have stopped Ellen before going on the elevator and repeated the tapping procedures. In this case, I didn't get a chance because she quickly entered an open elevator and began pushing the buttons with an obvious sense of glee.

I got in with her just as the doors were closing and we spent the next ten minutes in that elevator. We went up, down, stopped, resumed, opened the doors, closed the doors, and tested her fear in every way we could. She was totally relaxed, with not even a trace of her lifelong fear.

Once again I had the privilege of handing someone the keys to emotional freedom, just as I did for our Vietnam veterans and in the other case histories you have been exposed to in this manual.

You are on your way to gaining the same ability. (To expand your understanding of EFT, the videos and audios listed in appendix C offer still more case histories.)

EFT Part II

This part of the book assumes you have already studied EFT Part I and have persistently used the Basic Recipe for personal improvement.

What follows is the advanced portion of EFT. Here we get behind the inner workings of EFT Part I and expand our skills with this unique technique. In this section we will: (1) explore the impediments that sometimes inhibit EFT and learn what to do about them, and (2) take the Basic Recipe apart and learn some shortcuts for faster results.

There is much to be gained in these advanced areas and it is every bit as fascinating as what you have learned so far. But before going further, let's summarize the vital perspective you gained from Part I: The Basic Recipe is an extraordinarily powerful device even without the advanced details and if you persistently apply the Basic Recipe while tuning in to your problem, there is a good likelihood that the problem will fade away.

Although the advanced concepts are important for you to know, persistence with the Basic Recipe will often do the job. The Basic Recipe is a gift and is a condensation of many years of experience. Please keep this ever-present in your mind as you expand your knowledge in this section.

7

The Impediments to
Perfection

Even in the hands of relatively proficient newcomers, the Basic Recipe produces effective results about 80 percent of the time, particularly when applied to specific negative events in one's life. This is an extraordinary success ratio and few, if any, conventional techniques can make the same claim. An even higher success ratio is possible, however, when you know how to handle the impediments to perfection. There are four impediments that can hinder the results of the Basic Recipe:

- Aspects
- Psychological Reversal
- Collarbone Breathing Problem
- Energy Toxins

Impediment #1: Aspects

I include aspects here under impediments even though they are not actually impediments. They are apparent impediments because they seem to impede progress. Each aspect is simply a new portion of the problem that needs addressing before complete relief is gained. It is handled with the Basic Recipe just as if it is a separate problem (which, in a way, it is). If none of the other impediments are in the way, persistence will frequently neutralize the aspects.

Impediment #2: Psychological Reversal

EFT Part I introduced you to the Setup to address the more technical phenomenon known as Psychological Reversal (a term coined by Dr. Roger Callahan but originally brought to the public by Dr. John Diamond). Psychological Reversal is a fascinating discovery in itself and deserves special treatment in this book.

Have you ever wondered why athletes get into slumps? This defies logic. There is no physical reason for them to perform so far below par. The athlete is the same highly trained person before, during, and after the slump. But all athletes go through this many times in their careers. Why?

Have you ever wondered why addictions are so hard to overcome? After all, people trying to kick a habit want to be free of their destructive patterns. They know, and will often admit, that their addiction is costing them their health, their relationships, and even their life! Yet they continue with it. Why?

Have you ever wondered why depression is so hard to correct? It is one of the most difficult psychological

The Impediments of Perfection   125

issues to handle. People who seek conventional therapy to get over depression usually end up spending years and a lot of money on the process. And progress, if any is made, is usually accomplished in baby steps. Why?

Have you ever wondered why we sometimes sabotage ourselves? When we try, for example, to lose weight or read faster, we often manage to stop ourselves and fall back into our previous comfort zones with little or no real progress. Why?

Have you ever wondered why healing sometimes takes so long? The lingering cold that just won't go away, the sprain or broken bone that takes forever to heal, the headache or pain that stays and stays. Sometimes things just don't heal normally. Why?

The answer in all these cases lies in the body's energy system. A problem there is the actual cause of what is commonly called self-sabotage. It is the reason why we sometimes seem to be our own worst enemy and don't reach those "new levels" we truly want.

In addition to the previous examples, it is also why people often try in vain to make more money and fall short in countless other pursuits even though they know they have the ability to achieve them. It is also a contributor to psychological blocks (such as "writer's block") and learning limitations (such as dyslexia).

Before this discovery, people's seeming inability to make progress in areas of obvious importance to them was blamed on such things as lack of willpower, poor motivation, spacing out, or other forms of supposed character defects. But such is not the case. There is another cause, and it is correctable.

Psychological Reversal (PR) is that cause. It is an immensely important and practical discovery that is finding its way into various disciplines. Knowledge of it is vital in psychology, medicine, addiction recovery, weight management, and countless fields of endeavor including sports and business performance. Where PR is present, little or no headway will be made. It literally blocks progress.

What is Psychological Reversal? Everyone experiences it. It occurs when the energy system in the body changes electrical polarity, and it usually happens outside your awareness. You don't ordinarily "feel" it happening. It is a polarity reversal in your body's energy system, which is like having your "batteries in backward," as explained in Part I.

Interestingly, it often takes the form of what psychologists call "secondary gain or loss." For example, the person who consciously believes that he or she wants to lose weight will often have a subconscious "stopper" such as, "If I lose weight, I will only gain it back again and that will cost me a lot of money in changing my wardrobe." This person is psychologically reversed against losing weight.

How was PR discovered? Psychological Reversal has its roots in a field known as applied kinesiology. One of the tools of this discipline is known as muscle testing. Here the patient holds an arm straight out from the side of his or her body and attempts to keep it there while the testing doctor or other health care professional gently but firmly pushes down on it to assess the patient's strength. The doctor then has a dialogue with the patient and pushes down on the arm as the patient makes statements. If there is a subconscious disagreement with the statement, the muscles go weak and the arm is easily pushed down. Otherwise, the arm remains strong. This allows the doctor to "talk to the body" and thus help diagnose where problems might reside. Talking to the body can reveal the subconscious stoppers.

What causes PR? The principle cause is negative thinking. Even the most positive thinkers among us carry around subconscious negative, self-defeating thoughts. PR is the usual result. As a general rule, the more pervasive this type of thinking, the more prone we are to becoming psychologically reversed.

With some people it is an all-pervasive phenomenon. It stops them in just about everything they do. You can usually tell who these people are because nothing ever seems to work for them. They complain a lot and consider themselves a victim of the world. People with this across-the-board form of reversal are called "massively reversed."

PR is also a chronic companion of those who suffer from depression. Depression, negative thinking, and PR live in the same house.

Please understand that PR is not a character defect. People with PR suffer unknowingly from a chronic reversal of the electrical polarity in their bodies. Their energy systems literally work against them. As a result, they are continually stymied. It is not the world that is against them; it is their own energy systems. Their batteries are in backward.

Most people know, at least intuitively, that negative thinking blocks their progress. That's why there are so many books and seminars on positive thinking. Until now, however, no one has been able to explain how negative thinking creates these blocks, much less provide a way to correct it. Psychological Reversal explains the blocks and EFT provides a solution.

With most people PR shows up in specific areas. They may do very well in many areas in life but giving up cigarettes, for example, seems to be out of their reach. They may consciously and strongly want to quit. In fact, they may even give the habit up for a while. But eventually, if they have PR, they will sabotage their own efforts and start smoking again. They aren't weak. They are psychologically reversed.

The energy in our bodies must flow properly if we are to perform up to our potential. Psychological Reversal is one of the important ways in which it becomes interrupted.

PR is also correctable and the correction, which is called the Setup in EFT, only takes a few seconds to do. This process is covered in detail as part of the Basic Recipe in Part I.

PR is possible in any human endeavor. There are thousands of possibilities. But just to illustrate, the following are a few examples of Psychological Reversal.

Learning difficulties. Writer's block and most learning difficulties are often a direct result of PR. If a student does well in all subjects except one, the odds are high that PR is behind the poor subject. Students don't know they are psychologically reversed because, until now, they didn't even know the phenomenon existed. Instead, they tend to give reasons for their "inadequacy" such as "I'm just not cut out for chemistry," or "I can't seem to concentrate on it," or "I hate it." These reasons are usually inaccurate. The real reason is typically PR. When the students think about their poor subject, their polarity reverses and performance suffers accordingly. Correct the PR and the grades usually improve.

Some students are psychologically reversed about school in general. This is a major contributor to poor grades and it often goes unaddressed. The students are considered "slow" or "learning disabled." What a label to carry through life unnecessarily!

If you think about it, dyslexia is a classic example of reversal. In fact, reversal is its major symptom. Among other things, people transpose numbers and letters and thus have difficulty learning.

Annie approached me after one of my seminars and asked me if I could help her with the dyslexia she had lived with since childhood. She was forty-nine years old. She told me she couldn't write down telephone numbers accurately. "I get the first three numbers right," she explained, "but I mess up the last four."

I then recited ten telephone numbers to her in turn, asking her to write down each. Sure enough, all ten were wrong.

I helped her correct her PR and then recited ten more phone numbers. This time she got nine of them perfect, and it was effortless for her.

I don't want to leave the wrong impression. We may not have totally eliminated her dyslexia. What happened was that we got her Psychological Reversal temporarily out of the way and, with it gone, she performed normally. That is a stunning example of the power of PR. In the case of dyslexia, the PR will likely reappear in time and with it will return the dysfunction. Annie has more to do. But without an understanding of PR, her progress would most likely be very slow if, indeed, there was any progress at all.

Health problems. PR is almost always present with degenerative diseases such as cancer, AIDS, multiple sclerosis, fibromyalgia, lupus, arthritis, and diabetes. From an EFT point of view, it is one of the main impediments to healing. In time, I suspect Western medical disciplines will recognize this fact and integrate the correction of PR into their therapeutic techniques.

Unreversing oneself (aiming the Setup at a particular ailment) appears to allow the body's natural healing processes to work more fluidly. This makes sense when you consider the importance of the proper flow of energy throughout the body. Broken bones seem to heal more quickly when your "batteries are installed properly" and physical ailments of many kinds make greater progress.

Physicians, acupuncturists, chiropractors, and other health practitioners whose patients are making unsatisfactory progress might wish to teach their patients to unreverse themselves. It may release more healing force and speed up the recovery.

Poor athletic performance. It's a good bet that people are psychologically reversed whenever their progress is stymied in some area of their lives. Athletes are prime examples of this.

The great basketball player who is lousy on the free throw line is almost certainly psychologically reversed about shooting free throws. Correcting for the reversal will likely bring about a dramatic improvement.

The same goes for field goal kickers, high jumpers, batters, and athletes of all types that have a block of some kind in their performance. Owners and coaches of professional sports teams could make stunning use of the concept of PR and its simple correction.

Of particular importance with EFT is that when PR is present, the tapping procedure won't work. Remember, PR blocks progress and that is just as true with EFT as it is with any other technique.

I have many friends who are psychotherapists and they all have numerous clients that just don't respond to even the best of techniques. Until they learned of Psychological Reversal, this blockage was a mystery to them.

After years of experience with EFT we now know how often PR shows up. PR is present in about 40 percent of the issues that people address with EFT. In some issues, however, PR is almost always blocking progress. Depression, addiction, and degenerative diseases are the main examples. For most issues, however, PR may or may not be present in a given individual. For example, one person may be psychologically reversed for relieving asthma and another may not be.

How will you know if you are experiencing PR? You won't. That's why the Basic Recipe includes an automatic correction for it (the Setup). It takes only seconds to perform and it does no harm to correct for PR even if it isn't there. To repeat, unless PR is corrected, your success ratio with these methods will suffer dramatically. That's why the correction for PR is built into the Basic Recipe.

Impediment #3: Collarbone Breathing Problem

In a few cases, perhaps 5 percent, a unique form of energy disorganization occurs within the body and impedes the progress of the Basic Recipe. Its details are well beyond the scope of this manual, but I can show you how to correct it. I call it the Collarbone Breathing Problem, not because there is something wrong with the collarbone or the breathing of the individual who has this form of energy disorganization. Rather, it is named after its correction: the Collarbone Breathing Exercise.

Developed by Dr. Callahan, this correction need only be "thrown in" in cases in which persistence with the Basic Recipe is not showing results. It takes about two minutes to perform and may clear the way for the normal operation of an otherwise impeded Basic Recipe.

Collarbone Breathing Exercise. Although you can start with either hand, I'm going to assume you are starting with the right one. Keep your elbows and arms away from your body so that the only things touching are your fingertips and knuckles as described.

Place two fingers of your right hand on your right Collarbone Point. With two fingers of your left hand, tap the Gamut point continuously while you perform the following five breathing exercises:

1. Breathe all the way in and hold it for 7 taps.

2. Breathe halfway out and hold it for 7 taps.

3. Breathe all the way out and hold it for 7 taps.

4. Breathe in halfway and hold it for 7 taps.

5. Breathe normally for 7 taps.

Place the two fingers of your right hand on your left Collarbone Point and, while continuously tapping the Gamut point, do the five breathing exercises.

Bend the fingers of your right hand so that the second joint or knuckles are prominent. Then place them on your right Collarbone Point and tap the Gamut point continuously while doing the five breathing exercises. Repeat this by placing the right knuckles on the left Collarbone Point.

You are now halfway done. You complete the Collarbone Breathing Exercise by repeating the entire procedure using the fingertips and knuckles of the left hand. You will be tapping the Gamut point, of course, with the fingertips of the right hand.

How do you use the Collarbone Breathing Exercise? First, assume you don't need it and proceed as normal with the Basic Recipe. This is a logical assumption because this problem doesn't impede EFT for many people.

But if you have used the Basic Recipe persistently and your results are either slow or nonexistent, then start each round of the Basic Recipe with the Collarbone Breathing Exercise. You may find that it "clears the way" and allows dramatic relief.

Impediment #4: Energy Toxins

We live in a sewer.

Have you ever read the label on a bar of conventional soap? It lists chemicals most of us have never heard of. All those chemicals get into (through the skin and inhalation of the vapors) our bodies during a shower. We take in more noxious chemicals from standard shaving cream, hand lotion, toothpaste, and underarm deodorant. Then there are facial creams, hairspray, cologne, perfume, shampoo, cosmetics, and hair conditioner. The list of noxious chemicals that find their way into our bodies through such products is already intimidating, and that's just in the bathroom.

The water that comes out of our faucets contains another list of toxic substances. Yet we bathe in it, cook in it, and make our morning coffee with it.

Chemical residues from the laundry soap in which we wash our clothes come in contact with our bodies all day long. We sleep between sheets that have these same residues.

There are chemical air fresheners and deodorants in our homes and offices that may smell nice, but do so at the expense of filling our air with more chemicals.

At movie theaters, we eat popcorn loaded with rancid oil and salt. We drink soft drinks that are nothing more than chemical cocktails. We consume massive amounts of refined sugar. Our foods are laden with dyes, preservatives, and pesticides.

We ingest alcohol, nicotine, aspirin, antihistamines, and countless drugs. We breathe fumes from our cars, industrial smokestacks, and the insulation in our homes. In short, we face an army of chemical intruders twenty-four hours a day.

Like I said, we live in a sewer.

A different kind of "allergy." Our bodies are designed to ward off the effects of toxins and, all things considered, they do an admirable job. But enough is enough! Sooner or later, this onslaught shows up in our health. Allergies are among the most common reactions we have to all these toxic substances. Sores, rashes, and a host of sinus problems are but some of the allergic symptoms from which we suffer. Allergies are commonly thought to be chemically caused. That is, these toxins cause chemical reactions in our bodies, which are, in turn, responsible for our irritating symptoms.

But there is a different kind of allergy that needs to be introduced here—an energy system allergy. It doesn't necessarily irritate our internal chemistry and so it doesn't fit the classic definition of an allergy. Rather, it is like an allergy in that it irritates our energy system. For lack of a better term, we call the substances that produce this reaction "energy toxins."

Ways to avoid energy toxins. If you have repeatedly tried EFT with little or no success *and* you have exhaustively addressed all the aspects of the issue *and* you have applied EFT to the specific events that may be underlying the problem, then a possible culprit is some form of energy toxin that is irritating your energy system and thus competing with these procedures. It is not because EFT doesn't work. On the contrary, it works marvelously, given the proper environment.

There are several ways to avoid the effects of energy toxins even if you don't know what specific toxin may be affecting you.

Energy toxin avoidance method #1: Move from where you are. Sometimes there is something in your immediate environment that is causing the problem. It could be an electronic device such as a computer or TV or it could be fumes from a plant, carpet, or ventilation system. Perhaps you have some sensitivity to the chair in which you are sitting, or maybe the room you are occupying has been newly painted. So just the physical act of changing where you are can remove you from some offending item. You might want to stand up and go elsewhere in the room. If that fails, go to another room or go outdoors. Since EFT takes so little time to perform, you can move to several different places and try it out. If you find success with EFT after moving, then it is likely you have removed yourself from some toxin to your energy system. If you still have no success, then try the next avoidance method.

Energy toxin avoidance method #2: Remove your clothing and take a thorough bath or shower without soap. The clothes we wear have chemicals on them that may interfere with our energy system. The fabrics themselves can cause sensitivity as can the various chemicals with which they are manufactured. The chemicals used by laundries and dry cleaners as well as the residue from your laundry soap can also irritate your energy system.

You may have residues on your body from numerous other substances. Perfume, shaving cream, soap, cosmetics, hair spray, shampoo, conditioner, and so forth. My experience has shown that sometimes even a minute amount of a toxic substance is enough to cause a problem. Keep in mind that a substance that is toxic to your energy system may not be toxic to someone else's.

If any substances on your skin or in contact with your skin is interfering with your progress, taking a bath or shower and scrubbing vigorously with a soap-free washrag might correct the problem. Make sure you include sensitive areas such as underarms and the genitalia. Be diligent in areas where you may have applied perfume or cosmetics. Rinse your hair thoroughly. Washing in this way will usually remove the chemicals on your body.

Then start fresh with EFT. But this time, do it in the buff. I know that sounds a little odd, but this will often do the job. With all chemicals off your body, you minimize the chance of them interfering with your energy system. Make sure you stand up so that you avoid contact with chairs or beds or other possible offending substances. You will be barefoot, of course, and it would be best if you stood on a hardwood floor or a board or a piece of plastic. This way you avoid your carpet and any chemicals that might be in the fibers.

If this procedure results in success with EFT, then an energy toxin was likely in your way. If you still make no headway despite this effort, then try the next method.

Energy toxin avoidance method #3: Wait a day or two. If methods #1 and #2 don't allow the result you are looking for then, chances are the energy toxins aren't on you. They are probably in you. This means that the toxins were ingested through eating, drinking, or inhalation. If you wait a day or two, you allow the ingested toxins to be eliminated. And, once eliminated, they are not around to compete with these techniques.

If the ingested toxin is something you consume consistently, however, your system will, at best, have only small windows of time within which EFT can be successfully administered. If, for example, coffee is an energy toxin to you, then your everyday consumption minimizes the opportunity for EFT to work. It is forced to compete with an ever-present enemy within.

We are often addicted to the things we consume consistently, and thus giving them up presents a problem. EFT provides a valuable aid for those who want to get beyond their addictive cravings (see the case studies in Part I and my article on addiction in appendix A).

This brings us to an interesting point. Energy toxins are not always things that are commonly known to be bad for you. French fries, for example, fail to make the "healthy foods list" of just about every nutritionist in the country. But that doesn't mean that when consumed they interfere with your energy system. On the contrary, I often find that French fries a client has eaten are not in the way of these techniques. That still doesn't make them advisable to eat, of course. On the other hand, otherwise healthy foods can be very bothersome to your energy system.

As a general rule, things you consume a lot of will tend to be energy toxins to you. This is true even for the healthiest of foods, even lettuce. Lettuce, like all other plants, develops its own internal toxins to ward off predators. It is a natural form of self-preservation. We ingest these toxins whenever we eat the host plant. Normally, our bodies handle these toxins with ease. But if we eat a lot of lettuce, then we begin to overload our systems with these "lettuce toxins." These excess toxins then become bothersome to the body and, in particular, can irritate the body's energy system.

This goes for potatoes, peas, plums, and any other food that we eat. In short, foods we overdo become candidates to be energy toxins. It would be advisable to cut back on their consumption. While virtually anything can be toxic to your energy system, there are some food, liquid, and inhaled substances that show up with some frequency. The following may or may not be irritants to your system, but they are common energy toxins:

Perfume	Refined sugar	Alcohol
Coffee	Nicotine	Wheat
Tea	Dairy	Corn
Caffeine	Pepper	

How will you know which substances may be irritating your energy system enough to inhibit the Basic Recipe from working? You won't. But if you eliminate your ingestion of or exposure to all of the above substances for a week, the chances are excellent that the Basic Recipe will start working its wonders. If that doesn't do it, then ask yourself intuitively what might be an energy toxin to your system. Your intuition is often accurate.

Everyone experiences toxins, but that doesn't mean they will interfere with these techniques. On the contrary, most people are not bothered enough by the energy toxins to have them infringe on the marvelous procedures of EFT.

On the other hand, we must also be mindful that allergens or pollution cause some ailments. This is just common sense. EFT is often able to relieve the symptoms, however. In addition, EFT can sometimes eliminate the allergic reaction itself through using wording such as the following in the Setup affirmation:

- Even though I am sensitive to wheat, I deeply and completely accept myself.

- Even though I am allergic to my cat, I deeply and completely accept myself.

- Even though my soap causes a skin rash, I deeply and completely accept myself.

I've seen many cases in which allergic reactions completely disappear with the use of EFT. This is not always the case, but it is certainly worth a try.

Let me also mention that, in some cases, simply removing a given substance from the diet or environment can provide dramatic healing results. For example, one friend of mine had bouts of depression for many years. She took Prozac and other antidepressant drugs and had no real relief, only temporary masking of the problem. She eventually discovered that she was sensitive to wheat. Upon eliminating wheat from her diet, the depression lifted entirely. No pills, EFT, or anything else. Just the cessation of wheat in her diet.

The Value of Persistence

I started Part II of this book with the following reminder: If you persistently apply the Basic Recipe while tuning in to your problem, there is a good likelihood that the problem will fade away.

Persistence, by itself, can serve to sidestep the effects of many of the impediments to success with EFT. With persistence, you will be performing the Basic Recipe at different times of the day, indoors and outdoors, at the office, in the home, while wearing different clothes, and while enjoying different diets. This means your environment will be constantly shifting and you are likely to find one or more time windows where energy toxins (assuming they represent a problem for you) are not in your way.

In addition, if the Collarbone Breathing Problem is an issue for you, it is not consistently present. It comes and goes and persistence will probably find a time window for you where the Collarbone Breathing Exercise is not necessary.

And with persistence you are repeatedly performing the Setup and addressing aspects of issues you are treating, thereby routinely handling most problems presented by these phenomena. My point here is that persistence pays.

Diligently and persistently apply the Basic Recipe to whatever problem interests you and you will likely raise your success ratio without having to dwell on the technicalities of the impediments. Your success ratio will be even higher if you apply EFT to all the specific events in your life that may be contributing to whatever problem you are addressing.

8

Shortcuts

Since the Basic Recipe only takes one minute to perform, you might wonder why I would introduce the idea of shortcuts. After all, how much shorter than one minute do you need to get?

Although it is possible to skip this section altogether and still be very effective with EFT, delving into shortcuts gives you two advantages:

- You can deepen your understanding of the Basic Recipe because most of the shortcuts involve taking the process apart and detailing the individual pieces.

- Therapists, physicians, and other people helpers will appreciate the time efficiencies. You can often get by with a fifteen- or twenty-second version of the Basic Recipe and that timesaving really adds up if you are dealing with many clients. With faster sequences, you can also cover more territory with your client if there are multiple issues or issues that take multiple rounds to resolve.

Let's start the discussion of shortcuts by revisiting the Basic Recipe. It takes the form:

- The Setup
- Sequence
- 9 Gamut
- Sequence

If we can eliminate any of these steps or make them shorter, then, obviously, we gain some time efficiency.

Shortening the Sequence

The Sequence is the workhorse in the Basic Recipe. It is the main contributor to knocking down those emotional bowling pins after the Setup has prepared the way. Though we can't eliminate the Sequence, we can usually shorten it.

The energy meridians that circulate through the body are all interconnected. Experience has taught us that tapping on one meridian often affects another. Thus, through trial and error, I have found that tapping on fewer meridians usually does the job. I start with EB (beginning of the EyeBrow) and stop with UA (Under the Arm). Continuing on by tapping on the points of the fingers and hand is usually not necessary. I rarely do the entire Sequence. For clarity, the shortcut version of the Sequence, which takes only ten seconds to do, is as follows:

1. EB = Beginning of the EyeBrow
2. SE = Side of the Eye
3. UE = Under the Eye
4. UN = Under the Nose
5. Ch = Chin
6. CB = Beginning of the CollarBone
7. UA = Under the Arm

Eliminating the Setup

Please recall that Psychological Reversal is almost always present in depression, addictions, and degenerative diseases. Thus, in these instances, the Setup is almost always necessary to perform.

But in other cases, PR only appears about 40 percent of the time. This leaves an obvious 60 percent for which the Setup isn't necessary. Do we dare eliminate it and risk failure on the 40 percent in which PR is present?

Sure. There is a way to do it. However, I usually include the Setup because it only takes a few seconds to do. But if I choose to omit it, there is a procedure that allows me to know quickly if I need to go back and do it.

I start with the Sequence (the shortcut version) and then stop and assess if any progress has been made. I ask the person if the emotional intensity associated with the problem has dropped from the original number of, let's say, an 8. If the answer is yes, then I know the Setup wasn't necessary and I continue with the Basic Recipe.

How do I know the Setup wasn't necessary? Simple. I know that PR blocks progress dead in its tracks, and since progress was made in this example, PR could not have been there. If, on the other hand, no progress was made, then I must suspect that PR was in place and start the Basic Recipe over again, this time starting with the Setup.

With experience, you will find that some people have little or no PR to deal with. It's a delight to discover this because you can usually zip through their issues with incredible speed.

Eliminating the 9 Gamut Procedure

The 9 Gamut Procedure is not always necessary either. In fact, it is only needed about 30 percent of the time. I often eliminate it simply because 70 percent of the time it is useless. If I'm not making the progress I would like, I can always put it back in. If it was necessary, then progress should occur after using it.

The Floor to Ceiling Eye Roll

This is a useful shortcut when you have brought the intensity of the problem down to a low level, a 1 or 2 on the 0–10 scale. It only takes six seconds to perform and, when successful, will take you to zero without having to do another round of the Basic Recipe.

To perform it, simply tap the Gamut point continuously (while holding your head steady) and take six seconds to move your eyes slowly from hard down to the floor to hard up to the ceiling. Repeat the Reminder Phrase while you do it.

The Art of Doing Shortcuts

Because there is some art involved, it is difficult to put down on paper how to use these shortcuts in real situations. That is one reason I created numerous video demonstrations as a companion to this manual. Watching me use these shortcuts in numerous situations gives you a better feel for how to proceed. Experience is the best teacher when it comes to using shortcuts. This section simply acquaints you with the fundamentals. Please remember, however, that the Basic Recipe only takes one minute to perform. You don't really need to do the shortcuts. They are faster and more convenient, that's all.

Appendices

Appendix A: Articles by Gary Craig

Appendix B: A Format Diagram for Using EFT

Appendix C: Summary of the EFT Videos and Audios

Appendix A:
Articles by Gary Craig

Articles

Using EFT on Fears and Phobias

Using EFT on Traumatic Memories

Using EFT for Addictions

Using EFT for Physical Healing

Using EFT to Enhance Your Self-Image

Using EFT on Fears and Phobias

About 10 percent of the population suffers from one or more phobias. They can cause intense fear and often severely limit the lives of those who have them. There are hundreds of possible phobias and EFT can be effective on all of them. I include below some of the more common ones:

Public speaking
Heights

Snakes, spiders, and insects
Claustrophobia
Dentists
Needles
Driving
Elevators
Flying
Bridges
Rejection
Sex
Water
Speed
The telephone
Marriage
Men
Failure
Disease
Dogs
Computers
Bees
Being alone

What is a phobia? For our purposes, a phobia is any "excess fear" over and above normal caution or concern. Let me explain.

Our fears are essential, to a point. They are important to our survival. Without them we might walk off the tops of tall buildings, eat arsenic, or play tennis on the freeway. They are automatic mechanisms that kick into place when danger is afoot. They step on the brakes for us and keep us from harm.

But sometimes fears overdo their function. They go well beyond the normal boundaries of caution and create an unnecessary fear response. It is one thing, for example, to be cautious when you see a snake or a spider. Some of them are dangerous and could cause you harm. But it is quite another thing to experience a pounding heart, headache, nausea, vomiting, sweat, tears, or a long list of other excessive fear symptoms. These latter responses are useless in that they contribute no more to your safety than does normal caution. They are "excess fear" and serve only to create misery for the phobic person. It is that "excess fear," the useless part, the part above and beyond normal caution or concern, that we define as a phobia.

What is fascinating about EFT regarding phobias is that it eliminates the phobic part of the fear but leaves the normal caution or concern alone. People are often amazed at how quickly a lifelong phobia vanishes. But the process doesn't make them stupid. They don't suddenly jump off of tall buildings or kiss grizzly bears.

What is also interesting is that people who eliminate a phobia with EFT tend to have less fear than the general public with regard to that phobic circumstance. Almost everyone, for example, has some phobic response to heights. Ask a hundred people to look down from the top of a tall building and most of them will feel a little queasy. That's a phobic response, of course, but for most people it is rather mild. It doesn't cause them any real problem in their day-to-day living.

By contrast, those who completely eliminate a height phobia with EFT don't even feel queasy. They are left only with normal caution and could spend the day calmly looking off that building.

It doesn't matter how intense the phobia was or how long the person had it either. That's a big surprise to many people because conventional wisdom has told us for decades that long-standing, intense phobias are "deeply ingrained" and must take months or years to eliminate. Not so with EFT.

Some phobias take longer to resolve than others, but that's not because of their intensity or longevity. Rather it is due to their complexity, that is, the number of aspects involved.

If a phobia is being "stubborn" with EFT, try using EFT on the specific events that might underlie the fear. Examples are:

- Even though that snake bit me when I was eight, I deeply and completely accept myself.

- Even though I fell off the school roof in the fourth grade, I deeply and completely accept myself.

- Even though the class laughed at me when I forgot the words to my speech, I deeply and completely accept myself.

Consider now the Discovery Statement on which EFT is built: The cause of all negative emotions is a disruption in the body's energy system.

All phobic responses are negative emotions and are thus caused by a "zzzzzt" in your energy system. That means the solution to your problem is conceptually very easy. Just eliminate the "zzzzzt" and the phobia will fade to zero. No headaches. No pounding heart. No problems whatsoever. The emotional intensity will be neutralized.

The tool to accomplish this is the Basic Recipe. A few trips through it should eliminate the problem forever. How many trips you need depends on how many aspects there are to the phobia.

Aspects are important to address. In this case, the aspects are different parts of the phobia that contribute to the emotional intensity of the fear. Let's revisit the height phobia example for clarification on this idea. Most height phobics have had many specific events in their lives in which they were up high and their phobic responses left them with distressing memories. For example, one gentleman I helped with a height phobia had a fearful memory (aspect) of sitting on a water tower when a little boy. There was no way to get down and it scared him to death. Memories like this are separate aspects of a height phobia if, when separately recalled, they produce a fear response.

Since most phobias need only one aspect addressed, just one to three brief trips through the Basic Recipe will usually do the job. You will be rid of the problem in a matter of minutes and, in most cases, it will never return.

At this point, neither you nor I know how many aspects of your phobia need to be addressed. We can still proceed effectively. All we have to do is assume you have several aspects that need addressing and address them, one by one, until you have no more emotional intensity. When your emotional intensity has vanished, you will know that the process is complete and all relevant aspects have been addressed.

Questions and Answers

Q. Once the phobia is eliminated, is the result permanent?

A. Yes. If it appears to come back, however, that is almost always because there are aspects that weren't properly addressed the first time. If you then quiz the client (or yourself) on what is going on within, the person will usually speak about the fear differently. For example, the snake phobic might discuss his or her adverse reaction to the moving tongue of a snake. If this aspect didn't come up while using EFT, then it remains a problem. Using EFT on the moving tongue should eliminate that aspect and provide complete relief from the phobia unless, of course, there is yet another unaddressed aspect.

In other cases, a brand new traumatic experience could start the phobia all over again. In this case, you need only repeat the process again as if it were a brand new phobia (which it is). Relief should be moments away.

Q. What do I do if I have several phobias?

A. Address them one at a time. For example, make sure your spider phobia is totally neutralized before you address your claustrophobia. Then make sure your claustrophobia is totally neutralized before you address your driving phobia, and so on.

Some phobias are labeled complex in that they are several phobias wrapped into one. The fear of flying is sometimes like that because it can also involve (1) claustrophobia, (2) the fear of falling, (3) the fear of dying, (4) the fear of turbulence, (5) the fear of taking off, (6) the fear of landing, and/or (6) the fear of people. If you can isolate each in your mind, they qualify as different aspects and should be addressed separately.

If you have a complex phobia, but are unaware of it, persistent use of the Basic Recipe should still do the job. But it may take many trips through the process until all "zzzzzts" are neutralized. The intensity may rise and fall as the different aspects are handled "behind the scenes."

Using EFT on Traumatic Memories

(Including of war, accidents, rape, PTSD, and all past abuses)

In stark contrast to all conventional approaches, here we lump a nearly endless list of emotional problems into one category—traumatic memories—and handle them all as if they were identical. In fact, they are identical because they all have the same cause: a disruption in the body's energy system.

Traumatic memories generate a wide variety and intensity of emotional reactions when people recall them. People get headaches or stomachaches. Their hearts pound. They sweat. They cry. They may have sexual dysfunction, nightmares, grief, anger, depression, and any number of other emotional and physical problems.

Consider the Discovery Statement on which EFT is built: The cause of all negative emotions is a disruption in the body's energy system. Thus every negative emotion you have regarding a traumatic memory is caused by a "zzzzzt" in your energy system. That means the solution to your problem is easy, both conceptually and in practice. Just eliminate the "zzzzzt" and the emotional impact will fade to zero. No more nightmares. No more headaches. No more pounding heart. No more problems whatsoever. You will still have the memory, of course. But that is all. The emotional charge will be neutralized.

Our tool for this is, of course, the Basic Recipe. A few trips through it should give relief. How many trips you need depends on how many aspects there are to the memory. Aspects, as you recall, are different parts of the memory that contribute to your emotional intensity.

Most traumatic memories have only one main aspect. Thus one to three brief trips through the Basic Recipe will usually suffice. You will be rid of the problem in a matter of minutes and, in most cases, it will never return.

Some traumatic memories, though, have several aspects. They require more time because more trips through the Basic Recipe are needed. But even if extra trips are necessary, we are usually only talking minutes here. Maybe twenty or thirty minutes rather than the five or six minutes for memories without the additional aspects.

What we need, obviously, is a way to locate these aspects. Once located, it is a simple matter to address them one by one until every aspect of the memory has been neutralized. We can do this rather efficiently by using the "short movie in your mind" concept.

Consider a traumatic memory as a short movie that runs in the theater of your mind. There is a beginning. There are main characters and events. And there is an end. Usually, the movie plays in a flash and ends in a familiar unwanted emotion. Because the movie plays so fast, we are unaware that it may have different aspects that are contributing to the negative emotion. It seems to come from the movie as a whole. If we could run the movie in slow motion, the different aspects could be located and then addressed. So that is what we do. We run the movie in slow motion.

The best way to do that is to narrate the movie out loud. Tell it to a friend or a mirror or a tape recorder. Most important, tell it in detail. This automatically slows the movie down because words are much slower than thoughts.

As you tell it in detail, each aspect will make itself known to you. Stop as soon as you feel any intensity (remember, we minimize pain here) and perform the Basic Recipe on it as though it was a separate traumatic memory. Actually, it is a separate traumatic memory. It just got lost in a larger movie.

Then continue through the aspects, bringing each to zero, until you can tell the whole story with no negative emotional impact whatsoever.

As stated, most traumatic memories only have one aspect. Others have two or three. Rarely is there more than three, but it can happen. If that is the case, be persistent. Relief is not far away.

Questions and Answers

Q. What do I do if I have several traumatic memories?

A. Address them one at a time. Take your most intense memory first and bring it to zero before going on to the next one. Follow this pattern until all of your traumatic memories are neutralized. In the process, you will likely feel a freedom that can border on euphoria. It is an incredible gift to unload useless baggage like this.

Some people (such as war veterans) have hundreds of traumatic memories. If this is the case with you, you can expect the generalization effect to work for you. For example, if you have a hundred traumatic memories, you probably only need to address ten or fifteen of them. After that, you are likely to have difficulty getting any emotional intensity over the remaining ones. The generalization effect will have neutralized them.

Q. Doesn't the rapid elimination of emotional problems rob someone of the importance of exploring the problem in depth and getting to the bottom of it?

A. Conventional methods presume that the cause for these "deep-set" emotional problems resides in some recess of the mind that must somehow be discovered and excavated. To do otherwise is to "cheat" the client and leave the problem unresolved. EFT ignores this idea totally.

I have helped hundreds of people with traumatic memories, some of which were extraordinarily intense. After using EFT, not one person—ever—has shown any interest in exploring the issue further or "getting to the bottom of it." For them, it is completely resolved and they are gratefully relieved of its burden.

In my experience, EFT does get to the bottom of the issue and does so very powerfully. People's attitudes about the memory change almost instantly. They talk about it differently. Their words shift from fear to understanding. Their demeanor and posture evidence a dramatically shifted disposition toward the memory. They don't even bring it up any more because it has been put in perspective. All this happens when EFT removes the offending "zzzzzt" from the energy system. That's because the "zzzzzt" is the true cause.

Using EFT for Addictions

(Rethinking the Cause of Addiction)

Addictions are a mystery to most professionals. Addicted people who really want to be free of their addictions come to them for help. But despite their good intentions and despite spending a great deal of time and money, they usually revert to their former behavior.

When someone manages to kick one addiction, they typically pick up another in its place. Most people who give up cigarettes, for example, usually gain weight because they substitute food for cigarettes. Likewise, people who get beyond alcohol often resort to heavy use of cigarettes and coffee. In these cases, the addiction is not overcome; it is merely shifted.

The reason for the poor performance of most addiction treatments is that they do not address the true cause. If they did, people would not need to substitute one addiction for another.

So what is the true cause of addictive behavior? Let's start by listing what it is not. It is not what conventional methods have tried to make it for many decades. Thus:

- It is not a bad habit.
- It is not inherited.
- It is not because it runs in the family.
- It is not because the addict is weak.
- It is not a lack of willpower.

Though there may seem to be some logic in the proposed causes, which is why they persist, basing treatment on any of them has produced the same outcome: a poor record for relieving someone of addiction. What is needed here is the true cause, not a list of seem-to-be's.

The true cause of all addictions is anxiety, an uneasy feeling that is temporarily masked, or tranquilized, by some substance or behavior.

To many, this is a refreshing "aha" because it unveils a cause they didn't know how to articulate. Inwardly, they have always known that the need to smoke, drink, overeat, and so on is propelled by their need to tranquilize a level of uneasiness. But they didn't directly link that feeling with the true cause of their addiction. If you think about it, this link becomes obvious. Addicts often refer to their addictions as nervous (anxious) habits and addicts accelerate their use when under increased stress (anxiety). Take away an addict's substance (tranquilizer) and they will get very fidgety (anxious). In fact, they will often become anxious at the mere threat of taking the substance away. Listen to addicts when they talk about their addiction and you will often hear them say, "It relaxes me." This is the most obvious clue of all. Why would they need to relax unless they were feeling some form of anxiety? What else would they need to relax from?

Let's examine this further by looking at the false idea that addictions are just "bad habits." While there may be some habitual behavior involved, addictions are more than just bad habits. This is evident because habits, by themselves, are easy to break.

Here is an example. I have the habit in the morning of putting on my right shoe before my left one. If I wanted to change that habit it would be easy to do. I would simply put a note by my shoes that reminded me to put my left shoe on first. After a few repetitions of this process, my habit would change and the note would no longer be necessary. Changing a pure habit like this is easy because there is no anxiety involved.

But this same method would fail miserably if it were applied to the "habit" of cigarette smoking. Merely placing notes around to remind one not to smoke is a useless exercise. Those notes are powerless in the face of someone with an anxiety-driven craving.

When addicts have cravings, they seek out a favorite substance (cigarettes, alcohol, etc.) to tranquilize their anxiety. They do so, of course, in an effort to relax, calm their nerves, take their mind off of things, take a break, and so forth. All of these reflect different forms of anxiety, which is driving them toward the addictive substance or behavior.

So addictive behavior is not simply a bad habit. It is an anxiety-driven need that begs for relief.

The real problem for addicts is that their substance or behavior only relieves their anxiety temporarily. It merely masks the problem for a while. That's why it is a tranquilizer. When the effect of the tranquilizer wears off, the anxiety surfaces once again.

This is clearly so. Otherwise, one use of the addictive substance or behavior would permanently relieve the problem. As is well known, this is not the case. Instead, addicts must repeat their behavior for relief. They then grow dependent and end up associating anxiety with their tranquilizer. This becomes, of course, a vicious cycle in which they become trapped.

Often, their anxiety becomes even more intense when they are deprived of their tranquilizer. This increases their withdrawal symptoms and builds a barrier against giving up their addiction. The pain of withdrawal becomes too great a price to pay. They much prefer the risks of their addiction.

The Withdrawal Problem

This brings me to an attractive feature of EFT. It dramatically reduces the pain of withdrawal and often eliminates it entirely. This is but one of many features that set EFT apart from all other methods.

Withdrawal consists of both physical and emotional factors. When people discontinue an addictive substance, the physical need for it usually leaves within three days. This is a natural process whereby the body rids itself of unwanted toxins. But the emotional factor (anxiety) tends to persist for weeks or months and sometimes it never leaves.

In my experience, anxiety is the biggest part of withdrawal. This is obvious when you apply EFT because the anxiety usually subsides to zero in a matter of moments. And as the anxiety leaves, so do most of the withdrawal symptoms.

Let's turn now to the solution. Consider the discovery statement on which EFT is built: The cause of all negative emotions is a disruption in the body's energy system. Since anxiety is a negative emotion, it follows that it is caused by a disruption in the body's energy system. And that, of course, is easily addressed with the Basic Recipe. Eliminate the "zzzzzt" and you eliminate the craving. It's almost as simple as that.

I say "almost" because there is another important barrier to eliminating the addiction and the underlying anxiety: Psychological Reversal (see the section on PR in "The Impediments to Perfection" in Part II). PR applies in a major way to addictions. PR is the cause of self-sabotage.

It is the reason people thwart their own efforts and behave in a manner contrary to their own best interests.

All addicts know their addictive behavior is heading them in the wrong direction. Many try repeatedly to overcome it and, even if they make progress, they eventually defeat themselves by slipping back into their previous behavior. This is a classic example of PR.

PR is operational in more than 90 percent of all addictive behaviors. That is why we find it so difficult to put addictions behind us. Our energy systems change polarity and subtly work against our otherwise well-meant efforts.

That is also why we can eliminate addictive cravings and still find it hard to discontinue our addictive behavior. I know that may seem strange, but it happens consistently. If you have repeatedly failed to put an addiction behind you, I guarantee that PR is a major factor.

To be effective, then, we must eliminate both the immediate cravings and the Psychological Reversal. The Basic Recipe will be our tool, of course. It is particularly well suited to the task because it contains the Setup, a built-in correction for PR.

How to Address the Addiction

This is straightforward. Just aim the Basic Recipe at the addiction and repeat it throughout the day. It will help reduce any anxiety that is driving the addiction as well as correct for any Psychological Reversal.

The Setup does not eliminate PR permanently, however. It usually comes back and, in the case of addictions, does so frequently. Thus—and this is important—you will need to perform the Basic Recipe a minimum of fifteen times per day and I recommend twenty-five times per day.

This will keep your anxiety (and thus your cravings) at a low level and will continually keep the subtle (but damaging) effects of PR out of your way. In time, the PR should fade and diminish as a problem.

The twenty-five times per day should be spaced so that the tapping is done throughout the day. To do this you could: (1) get a watch that beeps every half hour to remind you to tap, or (2) do the tapping along with habitual daily routines such as:

- When you get up in the morning.
- When you go to bed at night.
- Before each meal.
- Every time you walk into the bathroom.
- Every time you get into or out of a car.
- Every time you hang up the telephone.
- Every time you sit down.
- Every time you stand up.
- Every time you enter or leave your house.
- Every time you go through a doorway.

Obviously, people have different routines and some of these may not be practical for you. They are listed to give you the idea. Customize your own list for your circumstances.

Sometimes you will find yourself in social circumstances (such as at parties or in restaurants) in which doing the Basic Recipe may cause others to doubt your sanity. In that case, excuse yourself and go into the bathroom or out to your car or anyplace else convenient.

How to Address the Craving

If you follow the previous precisely, it is unlikely that you will have much in the way of withdrawal or cravings during the day. But if you do, you must perform one or more rounds of the Basic Recipe until the craving subsides. This is in addition to the recommended twenty-five repetitions for the addiction.

Addressing Specific Events That Cause Your Anxiety

Though the previous routine, if followed diligently, should assist you in breaking an addiction, I must also, in the interest of thoroughness, urge you to address the specific events underlying the anxieties that addictive behaviors strive to tranquilize.

Seemingly, this can be a daunting process because most people are not aware of the specific events that contribute directly to the addictive behavior. So, without that awareness, how can they apply EFT? Also, depending on the person, there may be an endless list of such specific events.

The Personal Peace Procedure

Fortunately, there is a solution to this that I posted on the EFT website (www.emofree.com). It is called the Personal Peace Procedure. Its value here is to systematically collapse every specific event in your life that causes anxiety, addictions, or limits of any kind.

Properly understood, this technique should be the healing centerpiece for every person on Earth. Every physician, therapist, spiritual counselor, and personal performance coach in the world should be using it as a leading tool for helping others (and themselves).

In essence, the Personal Peace Procedure involves making a list of every bothersome specific event in one's life and systematically EFTing their impacts out of existence. By diligently do-ing this we can pull out every negative tree from our emotional forests and thus eliminate major causes of our emotional and physical ailments. This, of course, propels each individual toward personal peace, which, in turn, contributes mightily toward world peace.

Here are some uses:

- As "homework" between sessions with a physician or therapist. This is certain to accelerate and deepen the healing process.

- As a daily procedure to clear out a lifetime of accumulated emotional debris. This will enhance self-image, reduce self-doubt, and provide a profound sense of freedom.As a means to eliminate a major contributor (if not the sole cause) of a serious disease. Somewhere within a person's specific events are those angers, fears, and traumas that are manifesting as disease. Addressing them all will likely cover those responsible for the disease.

- As a useful substitute for finding core issues. Neutralizing all the specific issues will automatically include the core issues.

- As a means for consistent relaxation.

- To become an example to others as to what is possible.

This simple concept should shift the entire healing field. I can state it in a sentence: Most of our emotional and physical problems are caused (or contributed to) by our unresolved specific events, the vast majority of which can be easily handled by EFT.

Not bad for a mere engineer, eh? That sentence, if adopted by every healing practitioner and patient, would likely (1) dramatically increase our healing rates while (2) precipitously dropping our health care costs.

Please note that this idea completely ignores chemical causes such as those propounded by the medical model. That's because I have repeatedly seen improvements in clients for whom drugs and other chemical solutions have failed miserably.

This is not to say, however, that drugs, proper nutrition, and the like don't have their place. Indeed they do. They can often be vital. In my experience, however, our unresolved specific events are nearer the foundational cause for illness than anything else. Thus they deserve our primary attention.

How obvious! Experienced EFTers are well aware of EFT's ability to cleanly wipe the negative specific events off of our mental walls. This is the area wherein our highest success ratios appear. To date, however, we have focused our efforts on those negative specific events that underlie a given ailment such as a phobia, headache, or traumatic incident. This is good, very good, and we should continue doing so. On the other hand, why not use EFT on all the other specific events that are behind our more generalized (but very important) issues such as (to name a few):

Self-image
Anxiety
Depression
Persistent insomnia
Addictions
Compulsions
Feelings of abandonment

As you eliminate the emotional baggage from your specific events, you will, of course, have less and less internal conflict for your system to deal with. Less internal conflict translates into a higher level of personal peace and less emotional and physical suffering. For many, the Personal Peace Procedure results in the complete cessation of lifelong issues that other methods have not touched. How's that for peace in a paragraph?

The same applies to physical ailments as well. I'm talking here about everything from headaches, breathing difficulties, and digestive disorders to AIDS, multiple sclerosis, and cancer. It is becoming more widely accepted that our physical maladies are caused (or contributed to) by unresolved angers, traumas, guilt, grief, and the like. I have had many discussions with physicians in recent years and more and more of them echo emotional strife as a major cause of serious diseases. Until now, however, there hasn't been an effective way to eliminate these emotional health bandits. We can mask them with drugs, of course, but true cures have been hard to find. Fortunately, EFT and its cousins now provide easy and elegant tools that can aid the serious health practitioner in killing the root causes of disease, instead of the root causes killing the patient.

What I share here is not a substitute for quality EFT training nor is it a substitute for quality help from a masterful EFT practitioner. Rather, the Personal Peace Procedure is a tool that, properly applied, is capable of delivering wide-ranging relief (quality training or quality assistance add to its effectiveness). Its simplicity and far-reaching effectiveness give it candidacy as a mandatory method for anyone seeking help for even the most difficult of problems. I know that's a bold statement, but I've been at this for over a decade now and have seen so many impressive results over such a wide variety of issues that this statement is easy, if not essential, to make.

The Personal Peace Procedure is simple (I'm assuming you already know how to apply EFT):

1. Make a list of every bothersome specific event you can remember. If you don't find at least fifty, you are either going at this halfheartedly or you have been living on some other planet! Many people find hundreds.

2. While making your list, you may find that some events don't seem to cause you any current discomfort. That's OK. List them anyway. The mere fact that you remember them suggests a need for resolution.

3. Give each specific event a title, as though it is a mini-movie. Examples: Dad hit me in the kitchen. I stole Suzie's sandwich. I almost slipped and fell into the Grand Canyon. My third grade class ridiculed me when I gave that speech. Mom locked me in a closet for two days. Mrs. Adams told me I was stupid.

4. When the list is complete, pick out the biggest redwoods in your negative forest and apply EFT to each of them until you either laugh about it or it loses its charge. Be sure to notice any aspects that come up and consider them separate trees in your negative forest. Apply EFT to them accordingly. Be sure to keep after each event until it is resolved.

    If you cannot get a 0–10 intensity level on a particular movie, then assume you are repressing it and apply ten full rounds of EFT on it from every angle you can think of. This gives you a high possibility of resolving it.

    After the big redwoods have been removed, go to the next biggest trees.

5. Do at least one movie (specific event) per day, preferably three per day, for three months. It only takes minutes per day. At this rate, you will have resolved 90 to 270 specific events in three months. Then notice how your body feels better. Note, too, how your threshold for getting upset is much lower. Note how

your relationships are better and how many of your therapy-type issues just don't seem to be there anymore. Revisit some of those specific events and notice how those previously intense incidences have faded into nothingness. Note any improvements in your blood pressure, pulse, and breathing ability.

I ask you to pay conscious attention to these things because, unless you do, the quality healing you will have undergone will seem so subtle that you may not notice it. You may even dismiss it, saying, "Oh, well, it was never much of a problem anyway." This happens repeatedly with EFT, and thus I bring it to your awareness.

6. If you are taking medications, you might feel the need to discontinue them. Please do so *only* under a qualified physician's advice.

It is my hope that the Personal Peace Procedure becomes a worldwide routine. A few minutes per day will make a monumental difference in school performance, relationships, health, and our quality of life. But these are meaningless words unless others (you) put the idea into practice.

What to Expect When Using EFT for Addiction

As you apply EFT, your cravings should be dramatically reduced on the first day and should get milder and less frequent as the days roll on. Eventually, you should have no cravings whatsoever and any addictive substance involved will actually seem repulsive. You will be free. Your attitudes toward the addictive substance or behavior will change and you will wonder what you ever saw in it in the first place.

These are healthy signs, of course. When you reach this point, you should continue with the entire daily routine for a few days to "lock it in."

Once the addiction is broken, however, you are not immune to re-addiction. Avoiding any future temptation is advised. This is true, of course, with any addiction recovery.

Questions and Answers

Q. How much time will it take to get over my addiction?

A. This varies widely. In my experience, addictions to relatively mild substances such as chocolate, coffee, soft drinks, and various foods are often gone in a few days. I just finished helping a woman who overcame addictions to soft drinks, bacon, onion rings, chocolate, gooey type candies, and French fries. It took one or two trips through the Basic Recipe for each substance. She is no longer tempted by any of them. Other people take longer, of course.

Addictions to stronger substances such as cigarettes, alcohol, or cocaine usually take longer, maybe a week or two. I worked with one man who eliminated his several year addiction to alcohol in three or four trips through the Basic Recipe. This result is not rare, but it's also not the kind of thing I can predict for you. There are no hard and fast rules here. It is over when it is over. You will know when that is because you simply won't want the substance anymore. Withdrawal symptoms should be nominal.

Q. Can I address several addictions with the same trip through the Basic Recipe?

A. No. You can only address one addiction at a time. Do not combine two or more addictions in the same trip through the Basic Recipe. Use a separate trip for each addiction. Don't be surprised, however, if diligently pursuing one addiction breaks other addictions along the way. This happens sometimes because the tapping drops one's anxiety in such a manner that nothing is required as a tranquilizer. There's no way to predict this rather delightful phenomenon, but it does happen.

Q. How does EFT help with weight loss?

A. If you want to lose weight, you must address the foundational cause. And that cause is an addiction to food that is driven by anxiety, just like any other addiction. In fact, the number one addictive substance in America is food. It has a way of temporarily masking anxiety in a manner similar to tobacco and alcohol. How many times have you raided the refrigerator when you weren't really hungry? Why did you do it? To mask a feeling of anxiety? You may not have called it anxiety. You may have called it boredom or "nervous eating," but it was, nonetheless, a form of anxiety.

The anxiety that drives an addiction to food, or any other substance or behavior, can come from many places. It can come from stress in the family or workplace or it can come from abusive childhood experiences or traumatic memories.

To lose weight, obviously, you must eliminate the anxiety that drives the overeating behavior. What better tool to use than EFT? In addition to the Personal Peace Procedure, apply the Basic Recipe persistently (25 times per day) to your overeating behavior so that the underlying anxiety subsides. Use it again to reduce the unnecessary food cravings when they arise ("Even though I crave that pie, I deeply and completely accept myself") and, over time, the cause of your food addiction and thus your overweight condition should leave.

Using EFT for Physical Healing

Nowhere is there more obvious evidence for the existence of the mind-body connection than in EFT. By now you have witnessed (and I hope experienced) dramatic physical healing on several levels.

Here is a list of some of the physical ailments that have been addressed by EFT with either partial or complete success:

Headaches, back pain, stiff neck and shoulders, joint pains, cancer, chronic fatigue syndrome, lupus, ulcerative colitis, psoriasis, asthma, allergies, itching eyes, body sores, rashes, insomnia, constipation, irritable bowel syndrome, poor eyesight, muscle tightness, beestings, urination problems, morning sickness, PMS, sexual dysfunctions, sweating, poor coordination, carpal tunnel syndrome, arthritis, numbness in the fingers, stomach-aches, toothaches, trembling, multiple sclerosis.

There are many more. A complete list is several times as long.

Try it on everything.

I try EFT on every physical ailment presented to me and am repeatedly astonished at the results. I don't have 100 percent success (who does?), but EFT often gives startling relief when nothing else seems to work.

There are thousands of physical ailments that befall human beings for which the healing sciences have developed a wide array of remedies. These remedies range from a laying on of hands to drugs and surgery to fasting to mental imagery. They all seem to show results for some of the people some of the time. But none of them work for all of the people all of the time. EFT, in my experience, works so well that it should be included in every healer's tool bag. And I'll go a step further. I think it should be one of the first tools the healer uses. Here are the reasons:

- The relief from symptoms is usually immediate.
- It often works when nothing else will.
- It is easy to apply.
- It takes very little time.
- It is not habit forming.

I don't know any other healing technique that can make all these claims. Do you? Nonetheless, EFT does not replace medicine or any other healing practice. It is best to work with other healing practitioners.

That EFT deserves a prominent place in the physical healing hall of fame is undeniable. Even the most casual observer must greet the results with great respect. But the obvious question is: Why does it work? Why, if its original design is to address emotional issues, does the identical process work so remarkably well on physical problems? It is undeniable that negative emotions contribute to physical ailments. To the extent that EFT neutralizes those negative emotions, the physical symptoms appear to subside. In addition, just as the proper flow of blood throughout the body is vital to one's physical health, so is the proper flow of the body's energy. Thus, balancing it with EFT is bound to promote physical healing. There are many mysteries surrounding the healing sciences, which is why research in this field is an unending process. EFT is no exception and we can expect more information about this remarkable tool as research progresses.

Questions and Answers

Q. How long will it take to get relief?

A. There is no hard and fast rule on this. Symptoms often fade away in a matter of minutes, although, occasionally, there is a delayed reaction for a few hours. Relief from the underlying disease could take days, weeks, or months. So be persistent. And be sure to consult with your physician. Many people are tempted to discontinue medication as healing takes place. This should only be done under the guidance of your physician.

Q. Can I address several symptoms at a time?

A. No! Use the Basic Recipe on each symptom independently. Start with the most severe symptom and work down. Don't be surprised, however, if working with one symptom generates relief for the others. This happens frequently.

Q. Can I really expect results from EFT for long-standing, severe diseases?

A. I am quite aware that conventional wisdom suggests that many diseases of long duration are destined to be permanent fixtures in one's health profile. Accordingly, to suggest that they can be measurably reduced or eliminated by methodically tapping on the energy system is radical indeed. It is outside the beliefs of almost everyone I have met. But I have seen, firsthand, many startling examples of this and would be remiss if I didn't report them to you.

Q. How often should I apply the Basic Recipe to my problem?

A. For symptoms such as headaches, pain, and upset stomach, perform the Basic Recipe whenever you want relief. For the underlying disease, perform it ten times per day until you are satisfied with the results. The ten daily trips through the Basic Recipe should be spread throughout the day. A good way to do this is to develop the habit of doing them along with your habitual routines, such as:

- When you get up in the morning.
- When you go to bed at night.
- Just before each meal.
- Every time you use the bathroom.

It is also important to apply EFT to every specific event that might be causing or contributing to the physical ailment. Applying the Personal Peace Procedure will help as well.

Q. Will you please discuss some of your experiences with various physical ailments?

A. Sure. But please remember that the examples I give here represent a tiny portion of the possible ailments that EFT can address.

Back pain. I know many people who have significant damage to their backs and the reasons for their pains are evident in their X-rays. Nonetheless, after a few minutes of EFT their pains faded dramatically. This doesn't appear to make sense until you recognize that stress shows up in the muscles, which, in turn, exert abnormal strains on our joints. Relaxing the muscle tension, through EFT, thus reduces unnecessary stress on the joints. The result is less pain. I have lost count of how many back pains I have seen subside. Some pains vanish completely and never come back, whereas others require a daily tapping routine to keep the pain away.

Headaches and stomachaches. I estimate that at least 90 percent of the cases I have witnessed regarding these symptoms have responded very well. For most of them, the symptoms faded away completely within a few minutes of using the Basic Recipe.

Carpal tunnel syndrome. I had a business dinner one evening with Anne, whose carpal tunnel wrist pain was at a 7. After less than two minutes into the Basic Recipe, the pain disappeared altogether and didn't come back for the rest of our meeting. Needless to say, she was astonished since nothing else had ever given her relief. Our paths have not crossed since then, so I don't know how long it lasted. This is the type of problem, however, that tends to come back and so additional tapping would likely be necessary.

Psoriasis. Donna's psoriasis was so bad that she had difficulty wearing shoes. Her medications were not helping. She tapped routinely for a few days and 90 percent of it went away.

Allergies. These usually respond well. I have watched many people eliminate sinus drainage, itching eyes, sneezing, and a host of other allergy-related symptoms.

Constipation. Results vary widely here, but, in my experience, success is usually achieved. One person experienced instant and permanent relief with one tapping session. Others needed to tap daily for a few weeks before years of constipation was resolved. Please remember that you will not always get immediate relief from your physical ailment and sometimes the tapping will not appear to work. Be patient and persistent. All you are expending is time. The odds are in your favor if you keep with it. This applies to all ailments, not just constipation.

Eyesight. I have seen many people improve their eyesight with EFT, at least temporarily. People come up on stage with me, do the Basic Recipe for eyesight, and then report noticeably clearer vision. I have not carried through on this and cannot report on any permanent changes. I suspect, however, that permanent improvement is possible with persistence.

Arthritis. Arthritic pain often reduces under the Basic Recipe. I've seen this many times. Because of the underlying condition, however, it tends to return. Thus you must address the symptoms and the underlying disease. Can you reverse arthritis and get rid of it forever with EFT? I don't know because no one, to my knowledge, has persistently used these techniques for this purpose. Conventional wisdom tells us that arthritis is not reversible, that it cannot be cured but only arrested. I was diagnosed with arthritis in 1986, however, and have no sign of it today. I didn't use EFT at the time because I didn't know about it. It left as a result of fasting and changes in my diet, lifestyle, and frame of mind. I'm convinced that EFT would have hastened my cure.

Using EFT to Enhance Your Self-Image

The term "poor self-image" refers to a generally negative feeling about oneself. Authorities on the subject have not developed a precise definition for it nor have they pinpointed an exact cause. Accordingly, there is no agreed upon way to handle it.

EFT, by contrast, is much more precise in its approach and pinpoints an exact cause. Here it is:

The cause of a poor self-image is an accumulation of negative emotions about one's self. This is self-evident and is stated here because, in these terms, EFT makes eminently good sense. If we eliminate the negative emotions, then we eliminate the cause. And without the cause the poor self-image fades away. And what better tool to eliminate the negative emotions than EFT?

Poor self-image may be the world's number one ailment. It is so prevalent that almost everyone carries around some degree of it. Our self-image is often equated with our self-confidence. We tend to "radiate" it through our mannerisms, posture, words, and gestures and others pick up on it, whether we want them to or not. Accordingly, our self-image has a major effect on our business, social, and personal performance.

Sometimes jobs, promotions, and sales are won or lost depending on how we radiate our inner thoughts to others. Friendships and romantic encounters can flourish or die depending on how we project our feelings about ourselves. The lower our self-image, the easier it is to get upset and the more intense become our anger, guilt, jealousy, and other emotional responses. When our self-image is low we tend to stay stuck in one place. We don't venture into that new business or get out of that abusive relationship or try something new. Some parts of our lives can be very dull and depressing.

In short, our self-image is the centerpiece of our emotional strength. The quality of our lives often depends on it.

Go to the self-help section of any major bookstore and there you will find countless books with solutions to the self-image problem. In general, they emphasize positive attitudes and give exercises for looking at the brighter side of life. They encourage focusing on your strengths rather than your weaknesses and some emphasize visualization and affirmations to help you achieve these things. I applaud them all.

I'm in favor of anything that helps and many of these approaches do help people improve their self-images. The results are a bit spotty, however. An improvement here. A new attitude there. Rarely does anyone achieve an across-the-board, dramatically improved self-image with these tools.

The reason so many of these techniques fall short is that they do little to neutralize the self-doubt and negative feelings that make up the poor self-image. Rather, they try to overwhelm them with megadoses of positivism.

This is a laudable effort, of course, but one's established self-doubts and negative feelings can be rather stubborn. If your journey through life is like a bus ride, then these self-doubts and negative feelings are passengers on your bus. You are at the wheel and they are your "backseat drivers" who think they own the front seats. Conventional methods won't move them much.

EFT offers a refreshing new approach to this problem wherein dramatic, across-the-board changes do occur. I have seen people totally transformed by these techniques. Their mannerisms, posture, words, and gestures all change to reflect a more positive, self-assured person.

Their friends and coworkers comment on the "new" person that has evolved before their eyes.

Rather than try to install new attitudes and perspectives, as conventional methods tend to do, EFT effectively liberates people from their self-doubts and negative feelings. EFT loosens those unwanted passengers from their front-seat positions and kicks them off the bus. Once off the bus, they no longer contribute to a poor self-image.

The self-doubts and negative feelings that make up a poor self-image are forms of negative emotions, which, of course, are what EFT was designed to handle. Remember the discovery statement on which EFT is built: The cause of all negative emotions is a disruption in the body's energy system.

With this in mind, the process to improve your self-image is simple. Just perform the Basic Recipe on every negative emotion you have. One by one, they leave and, as they do, the balance between your positive and negative emotions shifts inevitably toward the positive. A refreshing and confident new self-image bubbles up to the surface. The unwanted passengers and their baggage have been thrown off your bus.

This is a perfect place to use the Personal Peace Procedure (see "Using EFT for Addictions" in this appendix). It automatically addresses all those negative specific events that intrude on an otherwise healthy self-image.

The Forest and Trees Analogy

Here's an analogy that will further help your understanding of this concept. Consider each of your negative emotions or specific events as a tree in a negative self-image forest. They might be reflective of things from your past like rejections, abuse, failures, fears, guilt, and so on. There may be hundreds of them and they may be so thick as to resemble a jungle.

Let's assume, though, that there are a hundred diseased trees in your self-image forest. If you cut one of them down (by neutralizing it with EFT), you still have 99 left. While you will get some noticeable, and much appreciated, emotional relief from removing that one tree, you still haven't made much of a dent in the self-image forest.

But what would happen if you methodically cut down one tree per day? Gradually, the forest would thin out. You would have more room to move within it and it would be a freer place in which to reside.

Eventually, with persistent use of EFT, all the trees disappear and in their place is a much more emotionally free you. The world looks different when the forest (or jungle) is gone and a new self-image emerges.

Fortunately, you will not have to cut down all one hundred trees to get your result. That's because using EFT to neutralize a few negative emotions of a given type will tend to generalize over the remaining negative emotions of that same type.

For example, assume that in your forest you have a clump of ten trees known as "abusive experiences." Take the biggest (most intense) trees in that clump first and cut them down with EFT. Once you have done three or four of them, you will usually find that the remaining six or seven fall on their own. Balancing the energy system for some trees then spreads to other trees of the same type.

You can then repeat this generalization concept with other clumps that might be called "failures" or "rejections." In this way, a hundred-tree forest might be cleared by cutting down approximately thirty trees.

Be an Observer

With EFT, shifts in self-image come much faster and much more powerfully than with conventional methods. But the shifts don't happen as rapidly as with phobias and distressing memories. EFT frequently handles those in moments, whereas a complete self-image change often takes weeks. This is because the shift in self-image is the result of the time-consuming elimination of numerous negative emotions (trees), one at a time or in clumps.

Although complete self-image change often takes weeks, change is under way throughout the process. With each tree that is removed from the forest, a shift in self-image takes place. The immediate emotional freedom that comes from the removal of that one tree, however, does not usually make a noticeable change in the much larger self-image problem. But the cumulative change that comes from removing several trees is noticeable if you become an observer of what is happening.

The changes that happen within you are gradual, subtle, and powerful. They feel so natural that you don't even realize that the shift is taking place. Eventually, your friends will comment on the difference in you and then you will have incontrovertible proof. But until then, you need to be an observer and tune in to what is going on with you.

Notice, for example, how you handled a recent rejection more matter-of-factly than before. Observe how you speak up more often and how you are taking better care of yourself. Listen to how the tone of your own conversation is shifting toward the positive. Watch the reactions of others toward you as you radiate a more assured self-image.

Being an observer is important because, without it, you might conclude that nothing is happening and give up on the process.

How to Proceed

The method here is simple. It is the essence of the Personal Peace Procedure. There are only two steps:

1. Make a list of every past negative emotion you can think of. Include every time you had fear, rejection, guilt, anger, abuse, tears, or any other negative emotion. Include both the big ones and the little ones but put the big ones at the top of the list. This is because you want to neutralize them first. Don't concern yourself if you can't think of every one of them at first. You can add to the list as they occur to you over time.

2. Then use the Basic Recipe every day to "cut down a tree" from your list. Do this daily until no more negative emotions (trees) exist. Be sure to observe your progress along the way. You can take more than one trip through the Basic Recipe per day if your schedule permits and you can cut down more than one tree per session. You must handle each tree separately, however. Don't lump them together in the same trip through the Basic Recipe. More than one tree may fall when you clear an incident of negative emotion, but it is not up to you to force that generalizing phenomenon. Simply focus on each tree.

After a few days into the process, you will notice that the "big trees" you started with don't seem to show up in your life any more. That is typical and there is a lot of freedom in that. Enjoy it.

Appendix B: A Format Diagram
for Using EFT

This diagram depicts a format, or flow, to use with EFT. It is a useful guide for knowing where you are in the process and becomes second nature after you have used it a few times.

BR = Basic Recipe; CBE = Collarbone Breathing Exercise.

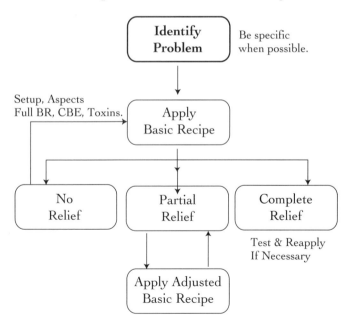

Appendix C: A Summary of the
EFT Videos and Audios

Videos and audios augment this manual to provide a more comprehensive EFT course. This manual teaches all the basics, whereas the videos and audios give you a visual/auditory experience of EFT in action and help you expand your skills. The videos and audios are available at www.emofree.com. They are part of the EFT Foundational Library. Also available through this website is a free subscription to our *EFT Insights* newsletter.

The Videos on DVD for Part I

Originally, there were three videos in Part I. Subsequently, the videos were put on DVDs (which dramatically lowered the cost). This necessitated breaking up the somewhat lengthy Videos 1 and 2 into DVD versions 1a, 1b, 2a, and 2b . It was not necessary to break up Video 3.

Video 1a

Here my colleague Adrienne Fowlie and I augment this manual by visually showing you each tapping point and how to perform each step of the Basic Recipe. We assume in this segment that you have already read the manual. Following along with Adrienne and me repeatedly can help you memorize the whole one-minute process. Once memorized, it is yours forever.

Video 1b

This is a complete demonstration of the entire Basic Recipe with a delightful gentleman named Dave, wherein we help him overcome a lifelong intense fear of water. Study this episode. Watch it several times. It is an excellent instructional session because it so well illustrates the handling of aspects.

Video 2a

This video features highlights of a workshop. The theory behind EFT is explained and then EFT is applied to two groups of people on stage. One group is dealing with fears and the other with pain.

Video 2b

In this video we show you more case histories of EFT in action. Here are highlights of what you will see:

- Larry: He overcomes intense claustrophobia while undergoing what would normally be his most tension-filled circumstance: riding in the backseat of a small car in the busy traffic of San Francisco.

- Pam: A chocoholic no longer wants her chocolate.

- Becci: Her fear of rats makes her hands sweat at the mere thought of one. She ends up having a live rat lick her fingers and says, "I don't believe I'm doing this. I am doing this."

- Stephen: A six-year-old boy is taught these techniques by his father and quits biting his fingernails.

- Adam: This is my son who uses EFT to knock fourteen strokes off his golf score.

- Cheryl: She shows up at one of our workshops and describes how I previously used EFT with her for her fear of public speaking. Our original session had been more than a year before and she reports that she has not had the fear since.

- Jackie: She had an accident ten years before that left her unable to raise her arm any more than a few inches without having intense pain in her shoulder. Within a few minutes on stage, she gets complete relief from the problem and can lift her arm at will without pain. This session shows our conversation after the workshop during which we discuss this "miracle."

- Cindy: Like Jackie, Cindy had an accident (three years before, in her case) that left her unable to lift her arm without pain. She had seen numerous physicians and therapists without result. In a few minutes with EFT, she lifts her arm as high as she can, with no pain.

- Veronica: With a heavy desire for a cigarette, she uses EFT to eliminate the craving. She then undergoes strong emotions about being raped by her father. After this one session, which you will watch in its entirety, she gets completely over this traumatic memory.

- Norma: She is dyslexic and has always needed to read things four or five times before she could understand them. She gets over that in minutes and later gets a new job that requires her to read out loud to people.

Video 3: 6 Days at the VA

This video shows highlights of our visit to the Veterans Administration in Los Angeles to help the emotionally disabled veterans of the Vietnam War. This puts EFT to the ultimate test because most of these soldiers have been in therapy for more than twenty years, with little or no progress. You will watch their emotional intensity melt away in moments. Nowhere is there a greater testimonial to the power of what you are learning. I mention this moving experience in my "Open Letter" at the start of this manual.

Important note about the videos: Please note that throughout Videos 2a, 2b, and 3, Adrienne and I use various shortcuts that we have learned over the years. With our extensive training we know when to shorten the process and we always do so in the interest of efficiency. Remember, we are usually dealing with skeptical strangers and are often doing so under difficult circumstances, that is, on stage. Accordingly, we use shortcuts (described in Part II of this manual) whenever possible and rarely do the entire Basic Recipe. Rest assured, however, that if we had taken the time to perform the complete process you learned in Part I, we would have achieved the same results. It would have taken a few seconds longer per round, that's all.

The main purpose of these video sessions is to give you a head start in the direction of experience by showing you how these techniques work in the real world, with real people, over a wide range of problems. The sessions take you out of the classroom and show you how these techniques are administered and how people respond.

Also, in some cases, some of the tapping has been edited out so that the session "moves along" on film. This allows the wider experience to come through without being burdened by the constant repetition of the procedures you have learned. I am not teaching the Basic Recipe on Videos 2a, 2b, and 3. That is done thoroughly in Part I of this manual and on Video 1. Videos 2a, 2b, and 3 are all about experience.

The Videos on DVD for Part II

Video 1: Overview

This video is a bridge between Part I and Part II wherein Part I is recapped and many of the new concepts in Part II of the manual are reviewed. Here we discuss the impediments to perfection, shortcuts, and the forest and trees analogy.

Video 2: Audience Examples

Videos 2 through 8 condense material from two three-day seminars. This video starts at the beginning of those seminars and explores a wide variety of issues, both emotional and physical, and illustrates the far-reaching power of EFT. It discusses issues such as the fear of public speaking, agoraphobia, anxiety, migraine headaches, physical pain, fear of flying, depression, fibromyalgia, and high blood pressure. There is also a discussion of the Discovery Statement and some important demonstrations of Psychological Reversal.

Video 3: Emotional Issues I

There are three sessions on this video:

- Jason: He works with anger and betrayal as a result of his wife leaving him and issuing a restraining order that prohibited him from seeing his daughter.

- Veronica: You will recognize her as the woman in Video 2b in Part I who used EFT on the traumatic memory of being raped by her father. She appears here, several months later, and still has no emotional problems with that specific issue. This is incontrovertible evidence of the power of EFT under even the most intense of issues. On this video, she works on a different issue. She has obviously intense emotions about being abandoned, alone, and unloved as a small child. Our session with EFT eliminates the problem and she comes back the next day to report that she feels "light as a feather."

- Sandhya: She works through her emotions regarding the experiences her father had during the World War II Holocaust.

Video 4: Emotional Issues II

There are two sessions on this video:

- Marlys: She uses EFT to get over "love pain," an obsession with the loss of romantic relationships. As this EFT session unfolds, several aspects show up and the issues shift in a daisy-chain fashion. The work eventually evolves into the fact that her mother didn't love her' after using EFT, she laughs about it.

- Kathy: She has three issues: (1) a fear of being touched (hugged); (2) a traumatic incident in which her mother threw boiling water on her; and (3) a sore shoulder, which is related to her having to fend off beatings. She responds beautifully to EFT, and the Setup to correct Psychological Reversal is not necessary even though numerous rounds of EFT are performed.

Video 5: Physical Issues

There are four sessions on this video:

- Connie J.: She has tightness in her jaw that comes from clenching her teeth while sleeping. The clenching is so severe that she has to wear a bite plate at night to protect her teeth. With EFT, she achieves complete freedom from this problem in minutes, even though it has been with her for several years. She also had a headache, which she eliminated on her own using EFT.

- Patricia: She comes on stage with an episode of asthma from which she has suffered for more than ten years. She gets dramatic relief with EFT and reports that it is still gone the next morning. She also experiences major relief from a back problem even though she has herniated discs.

- Dorothy: She comes on stage with an irregular heartbeat, an ailment for which EFT had not been used prior to this. Since we try it on everything, we applied EFT to it and substantially reduced her symptoms.

- Connie M.: She uses EFT for her neck pain, which, according to her, came about because of emotional issues. She gets complete relief.

Video 6: Addictive Cravings

This session starts with a conversation about addictive behaviors between two women who run an eating disorder clinic. Then follows: (1) an important discussion of the causes of addiction in the EFT model ; and (2) a session in which EFT is used on a group of people to overcome the immediate cravings for chocolate, cigarettes, and alcohol.

Video 7: Energy Toxins, Phobias, and Persistence

This video illustrates the effect of energy toxins and the value of persistence when using EFT.

The first part is an interview with Todd who gets nowhere during the seminar because energy toxins are in his way. He then comes back, a month later, to tell the members of another seminar about the dramatic effect a change in diet had on his sleep disorder, eye pain, and depression. Next is an unusual session in which several people experience improvement on their snake phobias. Though the improvements are dramatic by conventional standards, they are considered slow and relatively ineffective by EFT standards. This is due to suspected energy toxins in the room. Persistence is required to generate relief for most of these people.

Finally, we show the value of persistence in a session with Grace who was beset with intense depression and many other issues. We make little headway on stage, but her persistence and attention to her diet in the following weeks create major improvement in her emotional well-being. She tells of this with enthusiasm in a phone conversation.

Video 8: Common Problems and Q&A

This is a catchall video that explains EFT's use in such areas as sports (golf), business, public speaking, procrastination, self-image, and relationships. To round out your understanding, there is also a Q&A session with common questions from the audience.

The Audio Recordings on DVD for Part I

To widen your experience with EFT, there are several hours of case histories available on audio recordings. As with the videos, you won't be just listening to theory. These are real people with real problems. You will hear some people get over lifelong problems in moments while others require persistence. You will hear my colleague Adrienne Fowlie and me apply EFT to some severe emotional problems and listen to them disappear right on the audio. You will also hear of partial relief for some ailments. In short, these audios add to your rainbow of experience, thereby giving you a useful background that you can call upon when applying EFT.

Read the following points before you listen to the recordings:

- These audios contain a series of telephone sessions conducted by Adrienne and me. They are a collection of authentic sessions recorded with a desktop tape recorder. While the sound quality is certainly adequate, the recordings were obviously not made in the pristine atmosphere of a recording studio.

- Some of these sessions are with people who are actually undergoing EFT. As you listen, you will be an "observer" as people apply these techniques to a wide variety of emotional and physical problems. This will give you an invaluable "feel" for what you can expect when you apply EFT to yourself and others.

- Other sessions are with people who have used EFT in the past and are telling about their experiences since then. This gives you a good sense of the lasting nature of these techniques.

- The purpose of these audios is to expand your experience of these techniques. It is not to teach the tapping processes themselves. That is done by the manual and Part I Video 1a. Thus, as in Part I Videos 2a, 2b, and 3, I have edited out much of the tapping, so you can focus on people's responses and the other details involved in the techniques.

- You will be listening in on some highly personal problems and you will be doing so with the permission of those involved. They did it so others (like you) could benefit from these marvelous techniques. We owe them all a thank-you.

- Repetition is very important in learning. Accordingly, you will hear me repeat some important points, from different angles, many times during these recordings. This is not to bore you. It is to embed important concepts into your thinking.

- These sessions are for your education and not your entertainment (although some of them are very entertaining). I could have made them short and snappy by editing them to make a couple of quick points each time and then moving on. Doing so would rob you of some of the "feel" and "depth" to these processes. On the other hand, some conversations get off the subject and delve into areas outside the interest of this course. In editing these audios for your education, I have drawn a blend between these two extremes, erring on the side of including as much useful information as I can.

- Please note that the tapping you do hear on these audios will seem different from what you learned in this manual. It is not, in fact, different. It is simply shorter and takes a somewhat different form. As I mentioned in the section on the videos, Adrienne and I are advanced practitioners of these techniques and have been doing them for many years. Accordingly, we use some of the same shortcuts previously mentioned.

- There's another technique that is used in the audios. Adrienne and I have invested the time and money to learn Dr. Roger Callahan's Voice Technology in an effort to better assess the tapping points, the presence of Psychological Reversal, and other factors. We used this form of diagnosis on these audios to save time but are, at all times, using the same tapping points that you are learning. When I first learned Voice Technology, I thought it was a major aid in applying these procedures. After years of experience, however, I no longer believe it has material value and have discontinued using it. I have developed a more useful diagnostic technique, which is taught in great detail in our video set EFT—Beyond the Basics (formerly known as "Steps Toward Becoming the Ultimate Therapist"). Those interested in this advanced training should consult those videos.

- As previously stated, diagnosis is beyond the scope of this course. The Basic Recipe (using the 100%

Overhaul Concept) is being taught instead because it is an adequate substitute for the vast majority of cases. It takes a few seconds longer per round to perform and you may need to do a few more rounds (persistence) to get the same results. In any event, we are talking extra seconds or minutes here (per problem), not weeks or months.

- Listen not only to what people say, but also to the difference in their voices before and after using EFT. Also note that many times people emit a very relaxed "sigh" after tapping. This evidences the release of emotional burdens.On a few of the audios you will hear a "thump, thump, thump" in the background. This is the result of a malfunction in my tape recorder and is not someone's heart beating.

- You may be tempted to look at the "Session by Session Summary" below and go right to "your issue" on the audios. That's human nature, I suppose, but please don't ignore the rest of these audios just because they don't seem to apply to you for the moment. They contain valuable insights that will magnify your abilities with EFT.

Session-by-Session Summary

1. Barbara through Paulette

Barbara (7 min 35 sec): Relief from a traumatic memory (hitting a windshield), a headache, and insomnia.

Del (9 min 56 sec): He stands on a rooftop with a cellular phone and overcomes a lifelong, very severe, height phobia. The phobia is eliminated so completely that he goes skydiving. Neck and joint pains also subside.

Mike (3 min 28 sec): With graduate degrees in psychology, he finds this process astonishing. He gets over love pain (a breakup) very rapidly, but finds it hard to believe.

Ingrid (9 min 23 sec): She has had nearly constant irritable bowel syndrome distress, constipation, headaches, and "burning eyes" for many years. She gets substantial relief from all of them and becomes quite humorous about her constipation toward the end of this session. Paulette (4 min 40 sec): Lifetime fear of flying disappears. After EFT she takes two flights with no anxiety at all.

2.   Buz through Bruce

Buz (9 min 10 sec): A sufferer of a severe case of posttraumatic stress disorder (PTSD). Listen as he tells his most intense war memory as though it were a shopping trip.

Donna (1 min 35 sec): She uses EFT to help with her vision.

Kieve (9 min 45 sec): Pay particular attention to this one. Kieve learned these techniques just as you are learning them and applied them to 150 people with astonishing results. He tells of just some of the people he has helped with phobias, PMS, migraine headaches, hip pain, corn pain, and other problems. Master these techniques and you can do the same.

Cathy (7 min 23 sec): She has suffered from daily back pain since an automobile accident twenty-four years ago and has been through every imaginable method for relief, with no real help. She tells how the pain completely subsided after using these tapping techniques. She also dramatically improved her daily anxiety and insomnia.

Bruce (11 min 22 sec): He has had multiple sclerosis for seven years and gets noticeable resurgence of strength in his legs. He is confined to a wheelchair and stands up during the session. He gets feelings back in his hands and feet and reduces back pain and a sleeping disorder.

3. Geri through Bonnie

Geri (10 min 15 sec): This professional psychotherapist has a major fear of dentists. As it turns out, she has more fears than she thought. This session helps us understand that our fears and other negative emotions sometimes contain different aspects.

Shad (4 min 43 sec): He effectively manages daily stress and anxiety with EFT, and also uses the technique to improve his golf score by more than ten strokes.

Margie (3 min 50 sec): She reduces her addictive craving for chocolate to zero in moments. She says it doesn't even taste good now.

Mary (12 min 16 sec): She overcomes what she calls a global and planetary fear and reduces pains in her knee and back.

JoAnn (4 min 11 sec): She experiences the rapid elimination of throat discomfort and allergic symptoms.

Bonnie (8 min 38 sec): She has emotional disorders that keep her from swallowing food normally. In one session she overcomes some unidentified emotions and then swallows food easily.

4. Steve through Doris

Steve (13 min 0 sec): This sufferer of a little-known disease (hemolytic anemia) gets substantial relief from fatigue, heavy or itching eyes, back pain (with muscle spasms), and numerous other symptoms. He also eliminates an issue of anger and related nightmares.

Rachel (3 min 53 sec): She neutralizes the severe emotion of recalling a murder attempt on her by a boyfriend and gets over a breathing problem in the process.

Geoff (11 min 50 sec): He had seen five psychiatrists in the past but gained no relief from his depression. In two short sessions with EFT, the depression subsides.

Karen (6 min 17sec): She has fatigue caused by her insomnia and thus never feels rested. Relief occurs after one session with EFT.

Mike (7 min 50 sec): His extreme fear of public speaking dramatically improves. He reports that, after using EFT, he performed flawlessly in a presentation.

Doris (1 min 44 sec): A cancer patient, she tells of her emotional relief from using EFT and describes it as like having a "new body."

5. Bonnie

Bonnie (35 min 9 sec): She makes dramatic improvement in her self-image through persistent use of EFT. Bonnie had experienced numerous childhood abuses and had undergone conventional therapy for twenty-eight years at a cost of $50,000. She makes unparalleled improvement with countless traumatic memories, headaches, body shame, inadequacy feelings, fingernail biting, a phobia, anxiety, insomnia, and depression.

6. Jim through Dorothy

Jim (2 min 40 sec): His claustrophobia at being in a dark closet completely disappears in five minutes.

Patricia (5 min 11 sec): She goes from a 10 to a 0 on two separate aspects of the traumatic experience of being raped.

Juanita (1 min 57 sec): Her ongoing anxiety is relieved in moments.

Susan (2 min 12 sec): Pain from a back injury on the golf course goes away in less than a minute.

Geri Nicholas (9 min 28 sec): This professional psychotherapist appears for the second time on these recordings. This time she gives more insights into her personal use of EFT and how she uses it for others.

Dorothy Tyo (12 min 1 sec): This is a fascinating interview with a professional hypnotherapist who has used EFT, just as you are learning it, to help people with issues ranging from physical pain to the fear of public speaking to the fear of spiders to smoking to hiccups.